IT'S YOUR CLUB!

The Management of Sports Clubs

J.J. Killian

Published by Oak Tree Press, Cork T12 EVT0, Ireland

www.oaktreepress.com / www.SuccessStore.com

© 2021 J.J. Killian

A catalogue record of this book is available from the British Library.

ISBN 978 1 78119 515 4 (paperback)
ISBN 978 1 78119 516 1 (ePub)
ISBN 978 1 78119 517 8 (Kindle)
ISBN 978 1 78119 518 5 (PDF)

All rights reserved.

No part of this publication may be reproduced or transmitted in any form or by any means, including photocopying, recording or electronically without written permission of the publisher.

Such written permission also must be obtained before any part of this publication is stored in a retrieval system of any nature. Requests for permission should be directed to Oak Tree Press, info@oaktreepress.com.

Cover design: Kieran O'Connor

Cover image: Master1305 / Shutterstock.com

Disclaimer: The information contained in this publication is based on the author's personal experience and does not represent professional advice. Readers should always seek independent professional advice specific to their own requirements before taking any action based on the information provided herein. Neither the author nor the publisher assumes liability for any losses that may be sustained by use of the approaches outlined in this book, and any such liability is hereby disclaimed.

To Marian,
wonderful wife and best friend.

CONTENTS

		Figures	viii
		Abbreviations	x
1		**Introduction**	**1**
2		**The Operational Environment**	**3**
	2.1	What Makes a Club?	3
	2.2	The Sporting Context	4
	2.3	The National Sports Policy, 2018 – 2027	5
	2.4	Volunteering	6
	2.5	The Club in the Sporting Context	7
	2.6	Getting Involved in Your Club	8
3		**Club Structures**	**9**
	3.1	Legal Status	10
4		**Committees**	**11**
	4.1	Committee Structures	11
	4.2	Effectiveness of Committees	12
	4.3	Sub-Committees and Project Teams	13
	4.4	Membership of Committees	14
	4.5	Sample Agenda for a Meeting	15
	4.6	Types of Meetings	15
	4.7	The Annual General Meeting	16
	4.8	Conducting the AGM	17
	4.9	Activities between Meetings	18
	4.10	Committees in Action	19
5		**Club Officers**	**20**
	5.1	The President	20
	5.2	The Chairperson	20
	5.3	Chairing Meetings	21
	5.4	Secretary	22
	5.5	Treasurer	24
	5.6	Role of Members at Committee Meetings	26

6	**Governance**		**27**
	6.1	Corporate Governance	27
	6.2	Sport Ireland and Governance	28
	6.3	The Governance Code	28
	6.4	Governance and the Club's Constitution	29
	6.5	Club Documents to Support Governance	29
7	**Organisational Strategy**		**34**
	7.1	The Need for Vision & Strategy	34
8	**Leadership & Management**		**41**
9	**Marketing**		**47**
	9.1	The Marketing Mix	48
10	**Fundraising & Finance**		**51**
	10.1	Sports Capital Programme	53
11	**Operations & Administration**		**55**
12	**Planning Events**		**60**
	12.1	The Project Leader	60
	12.2	The Project Process	61
13	**Communication**		**65**
14	**Change**		**68**
15	**Organisational Behaviour**		**71**
16	**Growth**		**74**
	16.1	Growing Your Club	74
	16.2	A Roadmap for Change	76
	16.3	A "Club Within a Club"?	80
	16.4	Governance	81
17	**Conclusion**		**83**

Appendices

	1	National Governing Bodies & Representative Sports Organisations	84
	2	Club Constitution	85
	3	Safety Statement	100
	4	CoVID-19 Policy	103

5	Child Safeguarding Policy	105
6	Bullying & Harassment Policy	112
7	General Data Protection Regulations Policy	116
8	Garda Vetting Policy	118
9	Volunteer Policy	120
10	Complaints & Grievance Policy	122
11	Equality, Diversity & Inclusion Policy	124
12	Role of Welfare Officer / Designated Liaison Person	127
13	Job Descriptions for Key Roles	128
14	Financial Statements	132
15	Club Handbook	135
16	Strategic Plan	145
17	Marketing Plan	154
18	Planning an Event	158

About the Author   166

FIGURES

1	The Operating Context for Sports Clubs	7
2	An Example of a Club Structure	9
3	Unincorporated Entity v. Company Limited by Guarantee (CLG)	10
4	An Example of an Agenda for a Meeting	15
5	Sample Minutes of a Committee Meeting	23
6	Some Aspects of the Treasurer's Role	25
7	Some Aspects of the Governance of a Club	28
8	Strategy Management: Vision, Mission, Goals and Objectives	36
9	The Essence of the Strategic Plan	37
10	Strategy Management: Creating the Strategic Plan	37
11	Strategy Management: From Strategic Planning to Operations	39
12	Strategy Management: Operational Plan Template(s)	40
13	Management = Multi-tasking	43
14	Interaction between Leaders, Followers and Situation	44
15	Marketing Your Club 1	47
16	Marketing Your Club 2: The "One Cake" Approach	49
17	Club Operation and Administration	58
18	The Qualities Needed of a Project Leader	61
19	Planning and Organising a Club Event: The Process	61
20	Planning and Organising a Club Event: Timeline	63
21	Vertical / Lateral Communication	67
22	Building Commitment to Change	69
23	Club Management: Resources / Competences?	73
24	Club Growth Phases	75
25	Club Management: The 7S Framework	75

26	Club Operation and Administration	78
27	Running the Club	80
28	Governance – Club Structure	81
29	Overview of Your Club	83

ABBREVIATIONS

AGM	Annual general meeting
AOB	Any Other Business
CLG	Company limited by guarantee
CoE	Contract of employment
CRO	Companies Registration Office
CVC	Community, voluntary and charity
DLP	Designated Liaison Person
EDI	Equality, diversity and inclusion
EGM	Extraordinary general meeting
FAI	Football Association of Ireland
GAA	Gaelic Athletic Association
GDPR	General Data Protection Regulations
HSE	Health & Safety Executive
IRFU	Irish Rugby Football Union
LSP	Local Sports Partnership
NGB	National governing body
P&L	Profit & Loss Account
PESTEL / PESTLE	Political, Economic, Social, Technological, Environmental & Legal / Political, Economic, Social, Technological, Legal & Environmental (analysis)
PRO	Public Relations Officer
SCP	Sports Capital Programme
SPT	Strategy Project Team
SWOT	Strengths, Weaknesses, Opportunities and Threats (analysis)
WO	Welfare Officer

1. INTRODUCTION

Sports clubs are now operating in a more complex environment than ever before because club officers, committee members and general members have to be aware of a range of issues, such as governance, inclusion, diversity and current social legislation. Club members who just enjoy the sporting activities provided by their club may not notice much difference but, behind the scenes, those committed people who oversee their clubs know that the paradigm has changed and that their organisations have to be directed almost like a business and that every club member deserves to be considered in an all-inclusive environment.

There is a balance to be achieved here – the club must pursue its core mission of providing sporting facilities and promoting its chosen discipline – but it must now do so in a manner that reflects a set of values and an ethos that welcomes all sections of its community. In addition, it must conduct its business in a transparent way. The times when club committees operated in cocoons, stayed *in situ* well beyond their sell-by dates and conducted club affairs as if the members didn't exist, in most cases, have been consigned to the past. Most club officers and committee members understand that they have a duty to underpin the welfare and vibrancy of their clubs – their concern is that they might not always have the knowledge, skills or experience to carry out those duties.

The operational activities of working committees depend on the committee members to maintain standards and integrity in sports clubs. This may not happen in some situations, where some club officers never consider whether they have the skills required to carry out their responsibilities. A further problem arises in that sports clubs do not usually have any evaluation mechanisms in place – for example, formal internal audits – so it falls to individual members within a club to voice criticism of particular issues, often by way of comments from the floor during an annual general meeting (AGM). Sadly, there are many examples of clubs that get into difficulties because of inadequate stewardship.

Since, like governments, sports clubs are democratic entities, they are operated on behalf of the members by the officers elected to do so. There is, therefore, a clear responsibility on all concerned to ensure that good governance is applied to all situations in such organisations. The recent, well-aired travails of bodies such as the (then) Olympic Council of Ireland and the Football Association of Ireland provide case studies in how organisations can be damaged by myopic leadership and abject governance. Sports clubs must now take a more serious view of what they are trying to achieve and, to do so, they must have capable leadership, engage in good management practices, communicate more with the membership and create an inclusive environment that adds value to the social fabric of the local community.

2. THE OPERATIONAL ENVIRONMENT

2.1 What Makes a Club?

The notion of the "club" can vary from a group playing soccer on a public pitch every weekend, wearing a strip sponsored by the local pub, to the highly-structured GAA or rugby club, which may own significant facilities on its own land and may have a very sizeable annual turnover. However, the size or wealth of the organisation is not always what defines it as a "club"; many other factors must be considered, which will be explored throughout this book.

A group of people may form a sports club in order to involve themselves in a recreational, social or community activity that they all enjoy and they may never wish to move beyond that chosen position. However, it is difficult to see how that particular situation would perpetuate itself because different aspirations would eventually evolve within that group.

The ingredients that constitute a club include:

- **The Club:** A platform that enables a group or groups of people to identify particular sporting or recreational needs, to set goals in pursuit of such needs and to work together in a harmonious environment to satisfy such stated needs;
- **The Purpose:** Defining a purpose may not be as simple a task as it may appear. This implies the defining of a vision and mission for the club and clarifying objectives that all members can believe in and appreciate as being the means to achieving their agreed needs;
- **The Resources:** These depend on the nature of the club, on whether it has wealthy members willing to contribute to the common purpose, whether it owns property, what facilities it has access to, etc. The most important resource, however, for any club is its people, its members;
- **The Structures:** Structure depends on the purpose of the club – whether it needs multiple sub-committees, specialised facilities or more than one location, how are dispersed members catered for, as well as the number and size of committees;

- **The Relationships:** This can be the difficult part – catering for different needs, understanding particular dynamics, handling external bodies, maintaining a positive environment, managing conflict, organising communications channels, etc. Handle with care!

A club does not exist in a bubble – it has to be aware of, and adapt to, changing circumstances, internal or external. Having a good standing in the local community is critical to club development.

2.2 The Sporting Context

Most sports clubs in Ireland affiliate with the national governing body (NGB) for that sport, three key actors being:

- **The Gaelic Athletic Association (GAA):** The GAA is the largest sports organisation in Ireland and promotes the games of Gaelic Football, Hurling, Camogie and Handball. It is organised on an all-island basis and is viewed, not just as the keeper of the "national games", but as an integral part of social and cultural fabric of the country. Its competitions are organised on a club, county, provincial and all-island basis. Its basic structure is built on the "parish", although it has grown into one of the largest amateur sporting bodies in the world – one that has proven to be very astute in its strategic thinking. It faces its own challenges in that it continuously struggles with a huge competitive calendar, as well as issues over its amateur status;
- **The Football Association of Ireland (FAI):** The FAI is the body that oversees the game of soccer in the Republic of Ireland only, so it is not an all-island association. It runs soccer at various levels, from schoolboy level up to the national team. There are both amateur and professional sides to the game. The amateur leagues are organised separately to both the (professional) League of Ireland and the national squad, which is comprised of players who mostly play in Britain. Soccer, as with all other sports in Ireland, has to compete at every level with the GAA. However, it is hugely popular in every part of the country. The FAI has had its well-aired issues in recent times – many of which are concerned with governance – a topic that will be visited often throughout this book;
- **The Irish Rugby Football Union (IRFU):** The IRFU is an all-island body that governs both amateur and professional rugby in Ireland. The game in Ireland has been fortunate in that the four provinces provided a natural structure for the professional game. Rugby is driven from the top down by the national team, which provides the

2. The Operational Environment

main revenue stream, and is supported from the bottom up by the clubs and schools throughout the country. The All-Ireland League (AIL) provides an all-island competition for clubs of a particular standard, while the provinces schedule their own Junior Leagues. The academy system in each province now provides the pathway to professionalism and there is a growing gap between the clubs and the professional system. There are issues, such as the growing concerns regarding concussion but, that said, rugby is in a strong position and is growing in popularity.

The NGBs (see **Appendix 1**) support a huge range of sports, such as hockey, tennis, basketball, boxing, athletics, golf, swimming, equestrian sports, rowing, badminton, cycling, squash, motor sport, sailing, etc., etc.

There is now an overarching structure for sports in Ireland. The *Sport Ireland Act 2015* defines two strands of sport:

- **Recreational sport:** "All forms of physical activity which, through casual or regular participation, aim at — (a) expressing or improving physical fitness and mental wellbeing, and (b) forming social relationships":
- **Competitive sport:** "All forms of physical activity which, through organised participation, aim at — (a) expressing or improving physical fitness, and (b) obtaining improved results in competition at all levels.

Sport in general is overseen, and funded to various degrees, by the Department of Transport, Tourism & Sport. The Department then works with Sport Ireland, the Olympic Federation of Ireland (formerly the Olympic Council of Ireland) and the NGBs. Although all NGBs would state that they need more Government support, it must be acknowledged that such support has increased.

2.3 The National Sports Policy, 2018 – 2027

This document sets out targets for sporting achievement over the coming years, including:

- Overall participation in sport to rise from 43% to 50% of the population by 2027 (the equivalent of an extra 260,000 people participating in sport);
- More targeted high-performance funding to deliver more Olympic / Paralympic medals (from 13 medals in 2016 to a target of 20 in 2028);
- All funded sports bodies adopting the *Governance Code for the Community, Voluntary and Charity Sector* (see **Chapter 6**);

- NGBs organise, promote and facilitate opportunities for participation in sport and physical activity in both recreational and competitive forms. They train and deploy coaches, officials and administrators, organise representative level sport, provide opportunities and pathways leading from local sports to national and international competition, deliver critical national sports programmes in areas such as the safeguarding of children in sport, and organise the hosting of international sporting events;
- The Local Sports Partnership (LSP) network plays a similarly vital role and has been tasked, in particular, with increasing participation levels in sport and physical activity, especially among sectors of society that are currently underrepresented in sport. The LSPs' capacity to remove barriers and ensure that opportunities for participation in sport are progressive, innovative and fully inclusive at a local level is a unique and valuable strength;
- Representative Sporting Organisations play a vitally important strategic, operational and advocacy role for Irish sport at all levels. Their wide-ranging national and international perspective and expertise on issues affecting sport is a particularly valuable input to sports policy development. It is expected that the key bodies concerned – the Federation of Irish Sport, the Olympic Federation of Ireland, Paralympics Ireland, Ireland Active and the CARA Centre among others – will contribute to the National Sports Policy.

2.4 Volunteering

There are currently approximately 400,000 adult volunteers giving 3.5 hours per week on average to sport, a level of volunteering unparalleled in any other facet of Irish life. Its economic value has been estimated to be between €322 and €582 million *per annum*. It helps sustain approximately 12,000 sports clubs serving 1.7 million members.

Men dominate key management and leadership roles, such as coach and club official. Levels of volunteering decline significantly among older adults. Higher income earners and those with higher levels of education are most likely to volunteer. People's busy lifestyles tend to challenge time-heavy forms of volunteering and are driving newer forms such as episodic (once-off or time-defined) or micro-volunteering (park run).

Information about volunteering opportunities is not as widely available as desired. What is often raised in club conversations is the need to develop more generic training supports to deal with issues and challenges that might be common to volunteers across all sports.

Coaching is central to player development and to sports performance at all levels of competition and coaches are key agents in

2. The Operational Environment

ensuring a quality experience for existing and new participants in sport. Coaching is the main activity undertaken by adult volunteers in sport, with more than one in three of all volunteers regularly involved in this way.

There is a need to broaden the base of coaches. According to the 2017 *Irish Sports Monitor*, almost 70% of volunteer coaches are men, while 95% are white Irish. Coaching is also dominated by high income earners and individuals with a third level education. We need to ensure that Irish sport can involve all those with the initiative, skills and competencies to coach well. Broadening the coaching base to include more women, individuals with a disability and those from lower socio-economic backgrounds should help to stimulate a higher level of active participation among these groups.

2.4 The Club in the Sporting Context

It is beneficial for clubs both to understand and to be involved in the context provided by their NGB and the wider sporting structure. That context is shown in **Figure 1**.

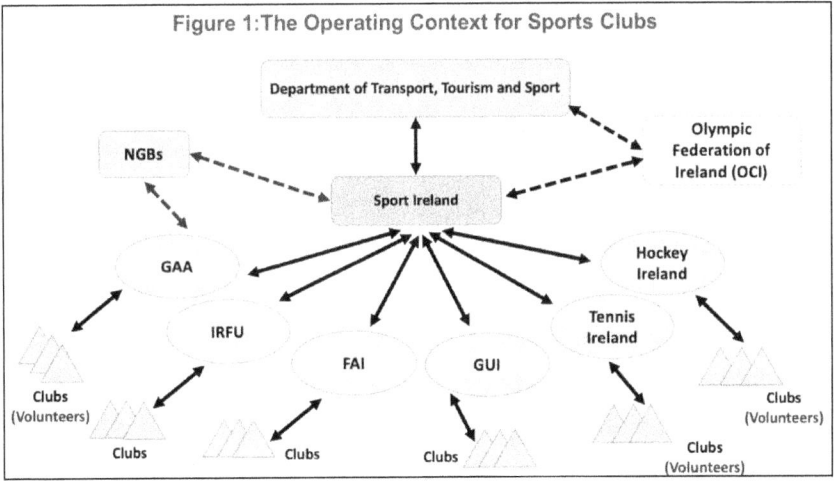

A club that has a vision and a strategy to achieve its goals will find its pathway to be less difficult if it engages with its NGB. This not engagement only builds awareness of what is achievable but gives the club a sense of partnership and a means of competing and collaborating on a bigger stage.

2.5 Getting Involved in Your Club

Every person who becomes a member of a club can exercise choice – to become a member and enjoy whatever facilities are offered by that club, or join as a member, enjoy the facilities *and* contribute to the operation of the club. Each choice must be fully respected within the club.

Before committing to involvement in club administration, you should consider:

- Do you understand and agree with the purpose and ethos of the club?
- Do you fully appreciate your own motivation for becoming involved?
- Are you willing to commit, give spare time and not be a "passenger"?
- Have you particular skills – in the sporting, administrative, fundraising or other areas of the club?
- Are you willing to begin as a club member and work your way up to committee and officer level?
- Can you articulate an argument, have a prepared opinion and be able to stick to your guns?
- Are you able to mix well with other people and tolerate other, often differing views?
- Do you think you have management or leadership skills?
- What are you going to bring to the situation?

The above list need not be too daunting as one is sharing the burden of running the club with fellow committee members who, presumably, are acting within structures that have been developed over time. The success of the club depends on how robust those structures are and on the commitment of the officers and the committee members.

3. CLUB STRUCTURES

Club structures can vary widely depending on their purpose and remit. **Figure 2** shows an example of a club structure, although some clubs have more complex structures and others simpler ones.

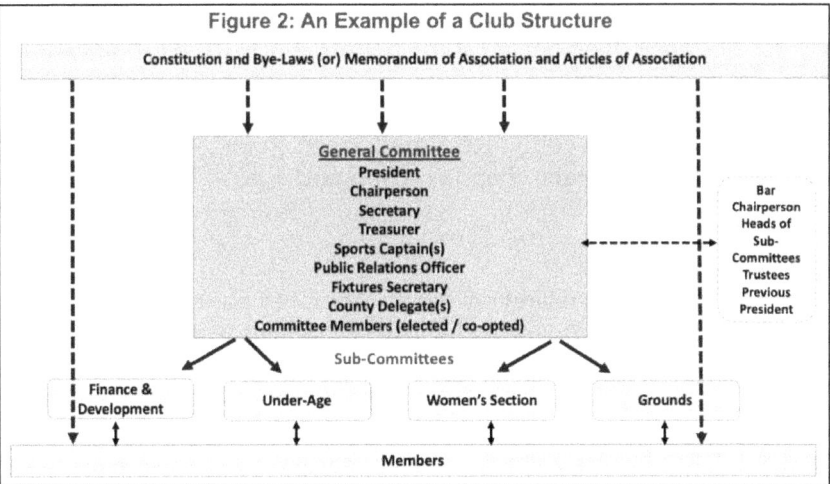

Figure 2: An Example of a Club Structure

There is no "one size fits all" solution to club structures – the best structure is the one agreed by the members to best suit the objectives of that club.

Structure depends on the size of the club, whether it is single-sport or multi-sport, whether it combines indoor and outdoor facilities, whether it has separate divisions (for example, golf clubs catering for Men's' and Women's' sections), etc. Clubs must also accept that such structures should be flexible and open to change – what was acceptable five years ago may not be suitable now. Business organisations always follow the *dictum* that "structure follows strategy" and clubs should adopt a similar approach because many large clubs need to be operated like small or medium enterprises (SME'). Regardless of the size of any club, the principles of good governance, astute financial management and transparency remain the same.

This view may clash with club members who "just want to get on with the sport" but the reality is that a medium-size GAA or rugby club probably has an annual operating budget in the region of €200,000 – more in the larger urban-based clubs. This places an onus on club structures and committees to conduct the club's business with prudence and due diligence. A club can no longer be "just about sport" if it wishes to survive and to compete at its designated level.

There will be a natural urge for growth in most clubs and that expansion will bring its own responsibilities – as well as a greater need for strong governance and astute financial management.

Business leaders like to tell us that "people are our most important asset". That's not quite accurate – having the *right people* is the key to growing successful organisations and progressive sports clubs are testament to that. This theme will surface often throughout this book – good clubs need good people at the helm. Every club has good people – they just need to be asked to help out. Some clubs are weak on this point – they often, sometimes unwittingly, give the impression that the committees and sub-committees are "closed shops". A club that wants to progress and embrace change must guard against this perception.

3.1 Legal status

Most sports clubs in Ireland are "unincorporated entities" – that is, they have not registered as limited liability companies with the Companies Registration Office (CRO). The differences between the two legal formats is shown in **Figure 3**. This book focuses on the unincorporated structure.

Figure 3: Unincorporated Entity *v* Company Limited By Guarantee (CLG)

Unincorporated Entity	Company Limited By Guarantee
Based on a Founding Document or Constitution.	Primarily governed by the *Companies Act, 2014*.
Assets / property usually held in trust by elected Trustees.	Operated by a Board of Directors who have fiduciary responsibilities under the *Companies Act, 2014*.
Operated by a General Committee elected at an AGM.	Must be registered with the CRO.
Can do anything that is legal and in line with the club's Constitution.	Must file annual returns with the CRO and Revenue Commissioners (unless granted charitable status, have surrendered VAT status, etc.)
Will have insurance in place, but personal liability of members is not limited.	Personal liability of members is limited.

4. COMMITTEES

I've searched all the parks in all the cities – and found no statues of committees.

(G.K. Chesterton)

Committees of all types in all organisations are easy targets for the hurlers on the ditch ("a camel is a horse designed by a committee", etc.). Despite this cynicism, there are always those who feel that they should give something back ... or just contribute because they can. Good clubs constantly trawl among their members to find new committee members and officers who will best suit the interests of the club. But that is often the ideal – committees can create strange dynamics and often attract people who definitely are not suitable. That is democracy in action so clubs must hope that they always gather in the best available talent. It is worth remembering that committees are cyclical by nature (and by the club's Constitution!) so a committee, regardless of its quality, is there for only a stipulated period.

4.1 Committee Structures

There are four aspects of committee structure to consider:

- **Legal structure:** The legal status of an organisation affect its structure – for example, the regulatory requirements of an unincorporated entity differs from that of a company limited by guarantee (CLG). Each club should examine carefully the implications of its legal status];
- **Evaluation of structures:** It may be necessary to adapt and reform structures as circumstances change or as the original set-up proves not to be suitable. Structures are put in place to support the work of the group – not the other way around;
- **Role of the General (or Management) Committee:** The General Committee has a joint and several responsibility to work towards the achievement of the club's objectives. To do this, it needs to coordinate planning, conduct evaluation, communicate effectively and act within the governance parameters of the organisation in terms of pursuing the aims of the club. The management

committee must always understand that it is accountable to the body of membership and all other stakeholders;
- **Membership of the General Committee:** Ideally, the members of the General Committee should collectively possess a range of skills and experience relative to the purpose of the club. A knowledge of the local community is definitely desirable, while the inclusion of people with business experience should definitely give an advantage to a club.

4.2 Effectiveness of Committees

The selection of a club committee usually results from a democratic process within the club.

Committees can be frustrating and ineffective when:
- They are unclear about their objectives;
- People opt out, don't turn up or don't contribute;
- Decisions are sewn up by a small group before the meeting proper takes place;
- There is a lack of clarity about what has been decided at the meetings;
- There is a lack of follow-up or action after meetings;
- There is a lack of preparation before meetings;
- The Chairperson is seen not to be in control.

Committees are more effective and welcoming when:
- There is a general feeling of inclusiveness;
- Everybody can hear, and understand, what is being said;
- Documents are provided beforehand if complex issues are to be discussed;
- Different communication styles are always accommodated;
- Members are representative of the club membership as a whole;
- Refreshments (tea / coffee / water) are made available;
- The committee is the correct size for the club.

In general terms, a good committee needs to have good *structure* and good *process*. A reasonable degree of formality is also required. Mustering good people and moulding them into an effective, coherent group can bring a club to another level, so every effort should be made to achieve this.

Going onto a committee can be a daunting experience for any club member – the club must understand this and make access to

committees more feasible. It could assist here by creating an "information pack" to be given to any new committee member. This folder might contain:
- The history and development to date of the club;
- The goals, objectives and general plans for the coming year;
- Financial projections and budgets for various areas of the club;
- Legal status – the club's Constitution;
- The role and responsibilities of the committee;
- Committee structure, sub-committees and relationships;
- Contact details of other committee members;
- Job descriptions for various roles in the club (for example, Hon. Secretary);
- Most recent annual report or minutes of previous AGM;
- Any particular issue(s) facing the club at that point.

4.3 Sub-Committees and Project Teams

It is very often necessary to set up sub-committees (under-age, grounds management, etc.) or project groups (building a new clubhouse, a fundraising scheme, etc.) but care is needed to ensure that the relationships between the General Committee and sub-committees are fully understood by all involved. Recommendations in this regard include:
- Be clear that the role of the sub-committee will contribute to the overall effectiveness of the General Committee;
- Be very clear about the purpose of the sub-committee so that conflict is avoided;
- If the sub-committee is, in fact, a project team, a time limit should be agreed for the completion of the project;
- Clarify exactly how, when, what and why the sub-committee / project team will report to the General Committee;
- Define the authority of the sub-committee / project team – does it have autonomy or does it have to receive permission from the General Committee before taking action?
- Decide on the membership profile of the sub-committee / project team by identifying the skills and experience needed for the task in hand;
- Define how and when the membership of the sub-committee / project team can be changed if required;

- Define how the critical area of finance is to be managed – it is always advisable that the Treasurer of the club is a co-signatory on any bank account opened by a sub-committee.

Clubs need to proceed cautiously in regard to the reporting structures for sub-committees. There have been cases where sub-committees and project teams were allowed to assume an autonomy and authority well beyond what was intended or envisaged, resulting in serious conflict and rifts within those clubs. In other instances, clubs have split apart and formed bitter rivalries – good communication, leadership and transparency can prevent such unfortunate outcomes.

4.4 Membership of Committees

Please accept my resignation. I don't want to belong to any club that will accept me as a member.

(Groucho Marx)

One cannot take Mr. Marx literally as clubs accept all types of people as members and rarely refuse an application for membership. Therefore, the constituency from which clubs can select committee members is predefined. But the members *are the club* so it is critical that the best available talent gets to serve on committees.

Clubs should identify individuals who would be seen as an asset, either in a sports or administrative capacity – this is a prudent approach, particularly if a club is seeking expertise which could be to its benefit.

Committee members are expected to:

- Be committed to the aims of the club;
- Be willing to work as part of the team in order to achieve those aims;
- Be prepared to take collective responsibility for decisions made;
- Be familiar with the club's rules (as in the club's Constitution);
- Be willing to engage in work or activities outside of meetings (for example, fundraising, meeting sponsors, organising activities, etc.) because practical actions have to take place.

Club members often think that they have nothing to offer on committees – but most people have skills that, combined with the skills of other members, can produce effective group synergies.

4. Committees

4.5 Sample Agenda for a Meeting

Templates for the agenda for a meeting are widely available – **Figure 4** shows an example, while other examples are included later in the book.

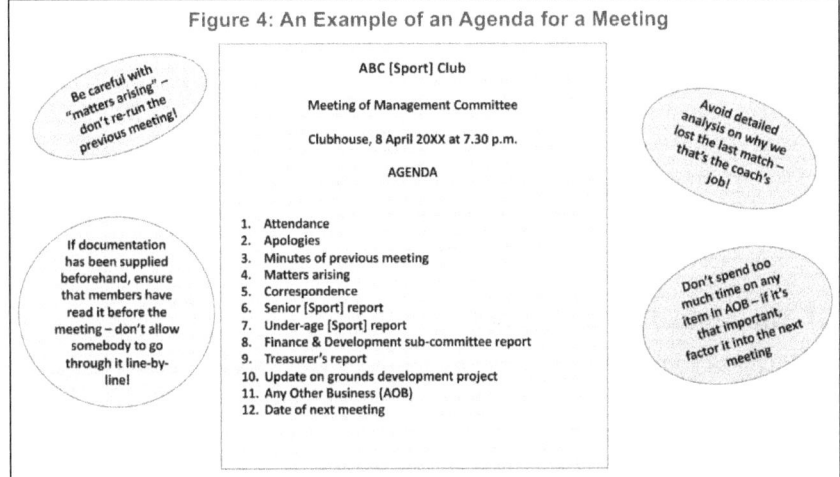

Figure 4: An Example of an Agenda for a Meeting

4.6 Types of Meetings

There are three main types of meeting:

- **Routine meeting:** Meetings of the General Committee (and other committees and sub-committees) should be conducted in accordance with the club's Constitution (which should specify the minimum and maximum intervals between meetings). In unusual circumstances, the chairperson may decide when a meeting should be held;
- **Annual General Meeting (AGM):** (Note that, if the club's legal status is that of a CLG, all meetings outside of the AGM are described as extraordinary.) AGMs are held annually to carry out particular functions:
    - To consider the Annual Report of the club (given by the chairperson);
    - To elect officers and committees to serve for the coming term;
    - To receive, assess and discuss the accounts (this confidential information should be collected again and remain within the club);
    - To receive annual reports from the various sports within the club;

    - To review and vote on amendments to the club's Constitution, should they arise;
    - To review and vote on proposals (if properly submitted and admitted) sent in by members prior to the AGM.
- **Extraordinary General Meeting (EGM):** An EGM can be called in a club if a specific number of club members or a specified proportion of the membership (the rules here must be clearly outlined in the club's Constitution) wish to address a particular issue. An EGM can arise if an issue cannot wait until the AGM – such an issue could be a vote on some significant expenditure by the club, a rule change that may have serious connotations, etc. The calling of an EGM should be neither too difficult nor too easy.

4.7 The Annual General Meeting

The AGM of the club, by definition, is held once per year so it is the most important meeting in the club's calendar and should be treated accordingly.

The AGM should be conducted strictly in accordance with the provisions as outlined in the club's Constitution – the Constitution needs to be precise in how it addresses this event.

There is often a perception in clubs that AGMs are boring, long-winded and peppered with dreary reports and financial figures that sail over the heads of those present. It's up to all club members to attend and to combat that image.

An AGM of a club should set the tone for that club – it should be properly planned and conducted strictly in accordance with the agenda. The Chairperson needs to be alert and be prepared to take charge of proceedings.

Any proposal, idea, amendment, etc. to be considered at an AGM should be submitted to the Hon. Secretary within the period specified in the club's Constitution (usually 14 days). Such proposals should be circulated, along with the agenda, to the attendance at the AGM. Proposals without notice, coming from the floor at an AGM, should not be entertained.

The "Any Other Business" (AOB) section of an AGM, usually the final item in the proceedings, should be managed carefully by the Chairperson and not allowed to become a platform for those who want to raise items that can be more appropriately handled at a routine committee meeting.

The sitting officers usually stay *in situ* until the AGM is concluded – the incoming officers and committee assume their roles at the first General Committee meeting following the AGM.

The serving terms of the various officers should be adhered to, regardless of how efficient the incumbents might be – if the term of a particular office is to be changed, it should be done on the basis of a proposal properly submitted prior to the AGM.

> *Great things are not done by impulse, but by a series of small things brought together.*
>
> (Vincent Van Gogh)

4.8 Conducting the AGM

The AGM of a club is usually held at a particular time in the sporting calendar – it is better if the date (or the latest date by which it should be held) is stipulated in the club's Constitution. The Secretary usually sends out notice of the AGM (by post, email, club website, social media platforms, notices in club, etc.) in time to provide adequate notice to the membership and to allow those who wish to submit motions to do so.

The sitting General Committee prepare the ground for the AGM and inform themselves as to which officers will stay on (if permitted by the Constitution) and whether there are suitable candidates for any positions that might become vacant. Lining up candidates for positions on a club committee is not to go against the principles of democracy – indeed, it would be naïve to arrange an AGM and hope that a suitable Chairperson, for example, will simply materialise from the attendance in the room. It is simply taking a practical approach to ensure seamless handovers and the smooth operation of the club.

It is normal practice for those attending an AGM to sign in so that the attendance can be recorded. A member of the public who is not a club member may attend the AGM but that person does not have the right to vote should a vote arise.

The most important person at an AGM is the Chairperson – a skilled chair will conduct an efficient meeting and keep the agenda moving.

The meeting usually runs as follows:

- Opening remarks by the Chairperson and reference to any guidelines to govern the occasion;
- Any apologies, documented or submitted through a member, are then noted by the Secretary;
- The minutes of the previous AGM are read by the Secretary – because of the time gap, these minutes should be read to the meeting and not "taken as read";

- Matters arising – any contribution here by any attendee should refer only to an item as read out and not be any other miscellaneous issue. Breaches here should be stopped by the Chairperson;
- Delivery of the Annual Report on the club's activities – delivered by the Chairperson;
- Delivery of the audited Accounts / Financial Report – this can be done by the club's appointed auditor or by the Treasurer in the presence of the club auditor;
- Reports from the Heads of Sports Sections, Sports Captains, Chairperson of Under-Age, etc. These reports should be given a time-limit – both individually and in total;
- Election of Officers for the coming year (stand down or retain office in line with constitution);
- Election of particular appointments (for example, Grounds Chairperson, Bar Chairperson, etc. Sports Captains can be elected by players after the AGM);
- Election of members to the General Committee (if insufficient numbers are elected, then the Committee may co-opt members when it takes office);
- Motions as submitted to the Secretary may then be aired – these may be accepted / defeated by votes if required;
- Any Other Business (AOB) – the Chairperson needs to be alert here – this item, if not managed, can be used as a platform by members who want to offer an (often lengthy) opinion or air some grievance. AOB should be tightly controlled with a view to bringing the AGM to a constructive and timely conclusion.

When it comes to electing officers at an AGM, it is better to avoid voting if possible. Voting can bruise egos, cause resentment, create cliques, etc. If a vote has to take place, then it should be conducted *via* a secret ballot. The AGM should be prepared and equipped (paper, pens, counters, etc.) for such an eventuality.

4.9 Activities between Meetings

Meetings can become "talking shops" unless action takes place between such meetings. Therefore, the Chairperson and Secretary should liaise soon after each meeting to undertake required actions – for example:

- Responses to correspondence can be undertaken by the Secretary or divided between the Secretary and Chairperson;
- Minutes of previous meeting to be written up and circulated if required;

4. Committees

- Liaison with any sub-committee in relation to projects in hand – for example, club Lotto, pitch upgrade, funding applications, etc.);
- Investigate the circumstances of any matter that may have arisen at the previous meeting;
- Check, after a short period, with any person who had been given a task at the previous meeting;
- Communicate with the appropriate people about arrangements for upcoming fixtures;
- Check with any persons / contractors who may be undertaking work at the club premises;
- Make enquiries about possible events – costs, insurance, resources, benefits, people, etc;
- Meet the club solicitor, club accountant, insurer, etc., in relation to any pertinent matters;
- Communicate with any committee member who may have had issues at the previous meeting;
- Arrange to meet current sponsors or potential sponsors regarding ongoing support;
- Oversee the planning for any significant project / event and liaise with responsible person.

4.10 Committees in Action

Matters discussed at committee meetings should always be regarded as *confidential*. The Chair should emphasise this regularly.

A *quorum* is the number of members of a committee who have to be physically present at a meeting to ensure that any decisions taken are binding according to the club's Constitution. A meeting will be *inquorate* if it doesn't have enough members to authorise its decisions.

It is always better to have the Chair of any sub-committee sitting on the General Committee – if this is not possible, then that sub-committee Chair should report regularly to the General Committee.

Committees contain extroverts, introverts, visionaries, realists, dreamers, organisers, tough minds, soft hearts, politicians and passengers. There are also those who love to play games. An efficient, no-nonsense Chair is invaluable. Be patient.

Don't be bullied! You were elected and have as much right as any other member to be there. Speak up – don't shut up!

5. CLUB OFFICERS

5.1 The President

The office of President depends on the organisation – in a voluntary organisation, the President is the face of the organisation and carries out specific functions whereas, in a sports club, the President might be either an honorary or an executive position.

Typically, a club President:

- Is elected at the AGM of the club for the period stipulated in the rules;
- Holds the primary honorary position in the club;
- Is the club representative at both internal and external functions;
- Is a member of the General Committee and contributes to policy creation;
- In the absence of the Chairperson, acts as Chair (if there is no Vice-Chair) at committee meetings;
- Provides liaison and communication channels between various sections of the club;
- Provides assistance or advice to members of the General Committee as required;
- Acts as a member of a sub-committee if this is deemed suitable and agreed;
- Contributes to the general standards of the club and provides an understanding of the club's ethos.

In some clubs, the Constitution stipulates that an immediate past President may sit on the General Committee – it simply depends on the club's rules.

5.2 The Chairperson

The Chairperson is usually (and should be) the most powerful and influential person in the club. He / she is elected at an AGM.

The Chairperson's responsibilities include:

- Holding primary executive responsibility for the everyday running of the club;

- Calling all meetings of the General Committee, AGMs, EGMs, meetings of specific sub-committees and ensuring that all such meetings carry out their tasks;
- Chairing the regular meetings of the General Committee and ensuring that its business is properly conducted;
- Liaising with the principal officers of the club and ensuring that they are carrying out their duties;
- Representing the club at internal and external functions in the absence of the President;
- Providing advice / direction to any sub-committee as required;
- Contributing to all policy-making decisions and to all decisions that may have significant financial implications;
- Monitoring the activities in the various sections of the club and ensuring that the club's espoused standards are being maintained;
- Maintaining close liaison with the Treasurer to ensure that all financial matters are being properly conducted;
- Acting as a mediator in the event that disagreement arises between particular sub-committees or sections;
- Carrying out the overall duties of the position of Chairperson in a manner that is befitting and in keeping with the ethos of the club.

All organisations need a discipline that makes them face up to reality.

(Peter Drucker, in *The Age of Discontinuity*)

5.3 Chairing Meetings

Chairing a meeting can be a daunting task, particularly if the General Committee has a normal attendance of 20 people or more. It takes practice so that confidence can be built up over a period of time.

Being fully prepared, calm and ready to get through the agenda is the starting point. A Chair who allows meetings to drift over hours will soon be confronted with a dwindling attendance.

So, at a meeting, the Chairperson must:

- Ensure that the meeting starts and finishes on time – long, winding meetings are not popular!
- See that the Secretary records attendance, as well as apologies from any non-attendees;
- Ensure that there is a documented agenda, with sufficient copies for attendees;

- If there is a particular issue to be addressed, highlight this at the start;
- Ensure that the agenda is adhered to (*do not let members go off on tangents*);
- Request the Secretary to read the minutes of the last meeting (*avoid the habit of "taking the minutes as read" – it's alright occasionally but it should not become routine*);
- Address matters arising from the minutes and request actions as necessary;
- Request the Treasurer to address the financial situation at the appropriate time;
- Go down through the agenda (*watch the clock – don't let any particular members hog the meeting*);
- Ensure that any person wishing to speak does so "through the Chair" (*do not allow cross-conversations*);
- Ensure that required actions are identified and agreed for each item and that tasks are assigned;
- Ensure that minutes are being recorded by the Secretary (or a nominated person in the absence of the Secretary);
- Summarise all decisions taken and wrap up the meeting

5.4. Secretary

The Secretary is elected at an AGM, or EGM. His / her responsibilities include:

- Acting as secretary to all meetings of the General Committee, AGMs, EGMs, and any sub-committee meeting, if requested by the Chairperson;
- Recording the minutes of all meetings that require their attendance, ensuring that such minutes are securely held and are handed over in good order to the incoming Secretary;
- Ensuring that all correspondence received by the club is brought to the attention of the General Committee and is subsequently held in similar manner to the club's minutes;
- Ensuring that all reactions / replies to incoming correspondence, as directed by the General Committee, are promptly attended to and that club headed paper is used in all such instances;
- Ensuring that correspondence initiated by the General Committee is promptly attended to and that it reflects the views / decisions of that committee;

5. Club Officers

Figure 5a: Sample Minutes of a Club Committee Meeting

Minutes of the meeting of ABC [Sport] Club, held on 15 September, 20XX.

1. **Present**
   J. O'Brien (Chair), S. Jones, (Secretary) M. Murphy, (Treasurer) R. Shaw, B. Dylan, P. Simon, S. Higgins, K. Doyle, I. Cooke.

2. **Apologies**
   L. Stokes, J. Ryan, B. Comerford.

3. **Minutes of previous meeting**
   These were read, approved and signed off.

4. **Correspondence**
   - Letter from [Sport NGB] outlining conditions regarding sale of match tickets.
   - Quotations from two companies relating to lighting on the all-weather pitch.
   - Invitation from Co. Council regarding a civic reception for the club.

5. **Finance**
   Treasurer outlined financial situation:
   - Current account balance stands at €14,856.00.
   - Lotto account balance stands at €18,300.50 – but current prize amounts to €9,500.
   - 1st Team medical expenses now running at €1,500 per month – up €300 per month on last season.
   - The new mower as discussed would cost €11,000 and a leasing arrangement is recommended.

Figure 5b: Sample Minutes of a Club Committee Meeting

6. **Payment of Annual Membership Fee**
   The Secretary raised the matter of annual membership fees, which were becoming more difficult to collect. After some discussion, the Chair directed the Secretary to inform all coaches that, with immediate effect, any person whose fee had not been paid could neither play for the club nor use its facilities.

7. **[Sport] Reports**
   Documented reports from both the senior section and under-age section were submitted. The 1st, 2nd and Women's teams were all strong seasons, while the under-age section was now able to field teams under every age group. The Chair complimented both sections on their performance and commitment.

8. **Volunteer Policy**
   Recent discussions on a documented Volunteer Policy for the club were referred to. K. Doyle, who had been tasked with writing this policy, presented a final draft. Having agreed to one amendment, the committee adopted the policy. K. Doyle will arrange, through the PRO, to have the policy uploaded on the club website and to have it otherwise circulated.

9. **Any Other Business**
   Following some discussion, it was agreed that:
   - The club would accept the invitation to the civic reception and organise a club group to attend.
   - A decision on the proposed design of the new club tie would be finalised at the next meeting.
   - A Life Membership would be conferred on A. Johnson, who had been a generous benefactor for a number of years.

   There being no further matters, the meeting was concluded. It was agreed that the next meeting would be held on 14 October at the clubhouse.

- Ensuring that all members are properly notified by post, or other agreed means, of any AGM, EGM or any particular meeting where the General Committee feel that a body of members is required;

- Controlling the acquisition of match tickets and ensuring that all match tickets are distributed strictly in accordance with any rules laid down by the General Committee from time to time (this task may be allotted to any committee member by the General Committee);

- Acting as an Officer of the club and providing advice / assistance to the Chairperson as required.
- Contributing to decisions and policy-making.
- After the AGM, notifying all categories of members, except Life Members, of the membership fee structure for the coming year and indicating the date by which such fees should be paid.

5.5 Treasurer

The Treasurer is elected at an AGM, or EGM. His / her responsibilities include:

- Ensuring that all financial matters relating to the club are properly controlled and recorded and that proper accounting measures are kept in place. Ensure that any sub-committee or section of the club that collects money in any fashion provides an account of same at the end of the relevant month;
- Providing a verbal report on the club's financial situation at each meeting of the General Committee and providing a written financial statement to that committee at the end of each calendar month.
- Contributing as an Officer of the General Committee to decisions and policy-making;
- Ensuring that all sub-committees provide a monthly statement of their financial activities;
- Reporting to the General Committee where this does not happen.
- Ensuring that all of the financial matters of the club are treated in a confidential manner;
- Reporting immediately to the Chairperson, if there is any doubt about any financial matter;
- Receiving all membership fees from the Secretary and lodging same in the appropriate account;
- Reporting to the General Committee on outstanding membership fees;
- Lodging all monies received from the various activities of the club to the appropriate accounts in the club's bank.
- Liaising with the club's bank, getting regular statements and checking that those statements reflect the club's financial activities;
- Allowing certain members of the General Committee to collect, record and lodge particular monies (for example, Bar, All-Weather Pitches, Lotto, etc.) on behalf of the club, but monitoring the bank statements to see that these are properly reconciled;

5. Club Officers

- Not allowing any Officer, sub-committee or member of the club to spend money or to commit to expenditure on behalf of the club without clearance from the General Committee.
- Ensuring that properly audited accounts are presented to the AGM and that explanations of aspects of the accounts are available to members.

A good Treasurer:

- Does not need to be a qualified accountant, but should have decent numeracy skills;
- Is able to appreciate the bigger financial picture in club terms;
- Is able to articulate the current financial position at General Committee meetings;
- Is a good organiser and communicator;
- Is enthusiastic;
- Is able to resist calls for impulsive spending that is not in the interests of the club;
- Creates a good relationship with the club's officers and auditors.

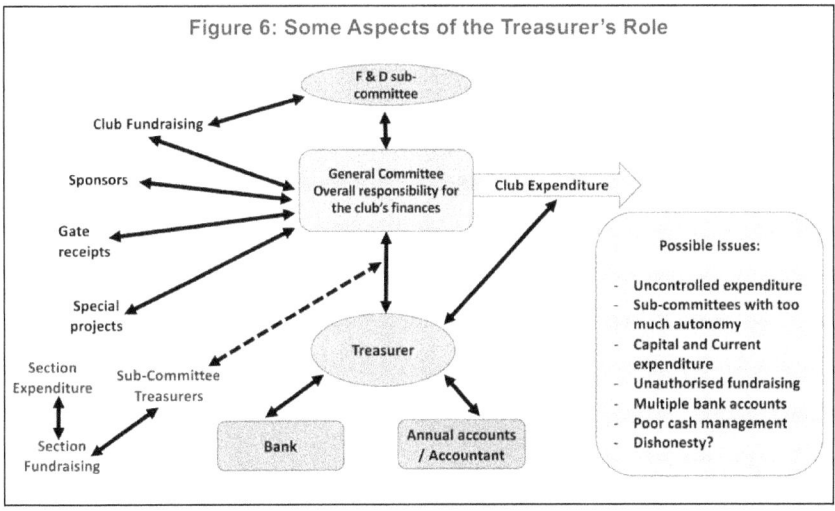

Figure 6: Some Aspects of the Treasurer's Role

Beware of little expenses; a small leak will sink a great ship.

(Benjamin Franklin)

5.6 Role of Members at Committee Meetings

All members of committees have a part to play in ensuring that committee meetings are successful. They should:

- **Be prepared for the meeting:** Read previous minutes, check agenda, be ready to raise any issue and have notes prepared;
- **Participate fully in the meeting:** Listen to others and process what is being said. Make points at the appropriate time. Be brief;
- **Be aware of feelings:** Work from the heart *and* the head. Be mindful of the feelings of others. Do not make personal remarks;
- **Listen to other views:** Avoid becoming entrenched – be prepared to be persuaded. It's about exchanging ideas and information. Show you are listening through body language and verbally agree with points to support people.
- **Assist the Chair in their role:** Support the Chair through good feedback. Don't interrupt. Speak through the Chair.

6. GOVERNANCE

Everyone can be great, because everyone can serve.

(Martin Luther King)

The debacle surrounding the former Olympic Council of Ireland (now the Olympic Federation of Ireland) and the Football Association of Ireland are ongoing reminders that sports clubs have a duty both to themselves and to their members to conduct their affairs in an accountable and transparent manner. These two situations also remind all committee and board members to speak out if they feel that there is anything amiss in their organisation. The members of a club *are the club*, so there is a collective responsibility to ensure that good governance applies to all activities within that club.

6.1 Corporate Governance

Corporate governance is the term usually applied to the proper operation of an organisation. It:

- Refers to how that organisation is run;
- Defines the techniques by which organisations are directed and managed;
- Means conducting the business of the organisation as per the wishes of its stakeholders;
- Involves balancing individual and societal goals as well as economic and social objectives.

Corporate governance is basically a detailed disclosure of information and an account of an organisation's financial situation, ownership, performance and a commitment to operational values and ethics. This affects all aspects of club operation as shown in **Figure 7**.

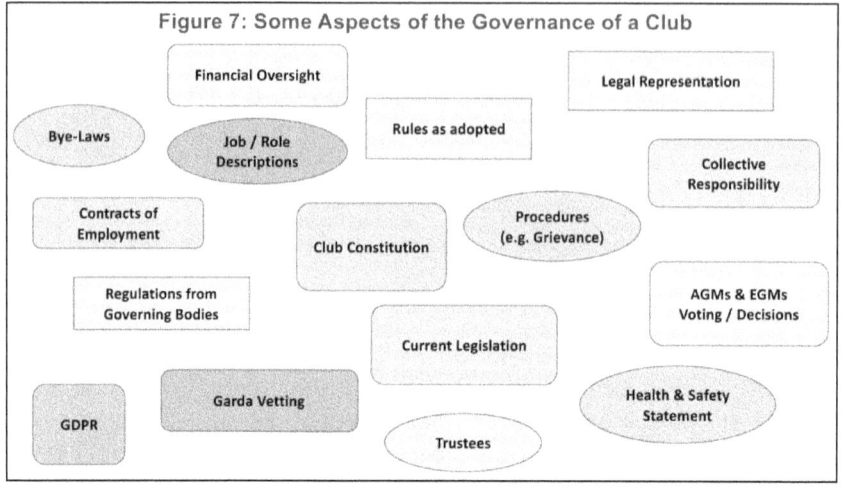

Figure 7: Some Aspects of the Governance of a Club

6.2 Sport Ireland and Governance

Sport Ireland has adopted the *Governance Code for Community, Voluntary and Charitable Organisations* as a governance code for sport in general in Ireland. This follows the decision of the Governance Code Working Group to retire the *Code of Practice for Good Governance of Community, Voluntary and Charitable Organisations*.

The Government's National Sports Policy, published in July 2018, tasks Sport Ireland with overseeing a process whereby all **National Governing Bodies for Sport and Local Sports Partnerships adopt the Code by the end of 2021 (Action 31)**. Through the *Governance Code,,* Sport Ireland can ensure that this objective is delivered and that all funded organisations have appropriate governance structures in place.

6.3 The Governance Code

The *Governance Code* was developed to assist community, voluntary and charity (CVC) organisations to develop their overall capacity in terms of how they run their organisations. It was a voluntary code provided free to all boards / committees / executives of not-for-profit groups to encourage them to check themselves against best practice in the management of their affairs.

There are five principles involved:
1. Leading your organisation;
2. Exercising control over your organisation;
3. Being transparent and accountable;
4. Working effectively;

5. Behaving with integrity.

Visit **www.governancecode.ie** and follow the six steps outlined there.
Note that sports clubs – the focus of this book – are classified as "Type A" Organisations.

6.4 Governance and the Club's Constitution

The Constitution is the club's reference point. It is advisable to avoid placing too much material in this document as it can be supported by other documents. Some points on this:

- The following items could be included in the Constitution or could be framed in another way (separate documents or placed in a club handbook, etc.) – Child Safeguarding Statement, GDPR, Bullying and Harassment Policy, Equality, Image and Rights, etc;
- The Constitution can be further supported by having "Job Descriptions" for the main officers of the club and for particular appointments such as "Club Coach", "Director of Rugby", "Grounds Chairperson", etc;
- Simple procedures for various activities can give life to actions required by the Constitution, provide clarity on various roles and prevent situations that can create conflict;
- The Constitution and other related rules should be available to all members – many organisations place their Constitution and other documents on their websites;
- The Constitution need not be regarded as "untouchable" – it can be amended / changed to meet evolving circumstances. Any change to the club's Constitution should be conducted at an AGM or EGM – on foot of a documented motion provided to the Secretary in a given timeframe as outlined in the Constitution;

One does not need a solicitor to write a club's Constitution – it's basic common sense – somebody in the club with good writing skills and an organised approach can write a Constitution. A suggested template for a Constitution is attached at **Appendix 2**.

6.5 Club Documents to Support Governance

Facts do not cease to exist because they are ignored.

(Aldous Huxley, Brave New World)

It is important, particularly in the current climate, that clubs have all the policy documents required to ensure good governance, to prove that current legislation is being complied with and to protect their members. This requirement should not be viewed as "nice to have" but as an important support structure for the club.

Setting up this structure entails some research and the creation of documentation. If this would be a burden on the Secretary, a club member with administrative skills could address this need.

It is recommended that, in addition to the club's Constitution, the following policy documents be established:

- **Safety Statement:** This document should directly address the particular Health & Safety issues in the organisation, so it should be tailored to requirements. The organisation should appoint a Health & Safety Officer – this person may already be a committee member. Some training may be required for this appointment. Health and Safety Statement and Risk Assessment templates are attached at **Appendix 3**;

- **CoVID-19 Policy:** The virus known as CoVID-19 is likely to be with us for some time, so it is advisable that every organisation should have a policy to provide general guidelines for members and to outline the actions to be taken in various circumstances. This policy can be adapted for use for other epidemics, if the need arises.. A CoVID-19 Policy template and a role description for a CoVID-19 officer are attached at **Appendix 4**;

- **Child Safeguarding Policy:** The existence of the *Children First Act 2015* should inform all clubs of the critical importance of safeguarding children who choose to use the facilities of their club. Such clubs are acting *in loco parentis* while children are on the premises or participating in club activities. This is now a core responsibility for any organisation that caters for children. All such organisations should have a child safeguarding statement as part of an overall safeguarding policy. The full requirements in this important area are outlined at **Appendix 5**;

- **Bullying and Harassment Policy:** Bullying is a form of harassment. Like harassment, bullying may have many motivations such as race, colour, gender, sexual orientation, etc. Clubs are now operating in more complex environments where particular behaviours, often practiced on the various social media platforms, can create sensitive problems for clubs and their members. Some such actions could contravene the equality legislation of 2004 so clubs have a responsibility to provide a safe, inclusive environment for their members. All the required information and a policy template are included at **Appendix 6**;

- **General Data Protection Regulations (GDPR):** Most clubs use websites and other media platforms to keep their members informed, to engage in marketing, to publicise events and for various other reasons. In doing so, such organisations necessarily use membership databases and other contact methods. This type of activity is now governed by the General Data Protection Regulations (GDPR). All clubs should have a documented policy in this regard; in addition, they should have a privacy statement, which should be placed on their website or other communication platforms. A policy template is attached at **Appendix 7**;
- **Garda Vetting Process:** The *National Vetting Bureau (Children and Vulnerable Persons) Acts 2012 to 2016* provide a statutory basis for the vetting of persons carrying out relevant work with children or vulnerable persons. The Act also creates offences and penalties for persons who fail to comply with its provisions. The Act stipulates that a relevant organisation shall not permit any person to undertake relevant work or activities on behalf of the organisation, unless the organisation receives a vetting disclosure from the National Vetting Bureau in respect of that person. It is vital that all clubs comply with this – a template is available at **Appendix 8**;
- **Volunteer Policy:** Most organisations would be unable to operate without the support of volunteers. There are now over 400,000 people giving personal time to clubs in this country so it is surprising that the majority of such organisations do not have a volunteer policy. It is strongly recommended that all clubs put such a policy in place so that there is clarity around what is expected from each party. A template is attached at **Appendix 9**;
- **Complaints and Grievance Procedure:** All clubs are comprised of people who interact in the pursuit of that organisation's activities. Such involvement may lead to behaviours which, for various reasons, might result in conflict or other situations that must be addressed by the club. It is therefore advisable to have a complaints and grievance procedure in place so as to be prepared for such an eventuality. This could be referenced in the club's Constitution or exist as a stand-alone procedure – it also could form part of an overall disciplinary code. A suggested template is attached at **Appendix 10**;
- **Equality, Diversity and Inclusion (EDI) Policy:** The environment in which clubs now operate is more complex and requires clubs to be genuinely open to embracing change and to acceptance of the new realities. A statement of non-discrimination in terms of membership should be included in the relevant section of the club's Constitution.

This expression can then be bolstered by having an EDI Policy – a suggested template is attached at **Appendix 11**;

- **Role of Welfare Officer / Designated Liaison Person:** The *National Guidance for the Protection and Welfare of Children, 2017* leaves clubs in no doubt as to their obligations in this respect. All organisations should have a welfare officer who can also act as the designated liaison person (DLP). This is an important appointment for the club and should be treated accordingly. There is a wealth of information pertaining to child safeguarding available from both the Health & Safety Executive (HSE) and Túsla. Some training will be required for this post – there are short courses available in this regard and it is strongly recommended that such training should be undertaken. A suggested template is attached at **Appendix 12**;
- **Job Descriptions for Key roles:** Most clubs have a range of officers, reflecting the form of organisation most beneficial to achieving its objectives. These officers are either elected or appointed in accordance with the rules governing the club. While there will be a general perception of the various duties involved in such positions, surprisingly most clubs do not have detailed job descriptions to outline the requirements of such positions. Some clubs will probably view this as being overly fussy but job descriptions for various posts clarify responsibilities, improve communications, outline the scope of the various appointments and avoid possible conflict. Suggested templates for key roles are outlined at **Appendix 13**;
- **Financial Statements:** Clubs that receive public funding usually are required to publish annual accounts. This can be done by simply uploading the financial statements onto the organisation's website or by other chosen means. Sports clubs in general, unless they are set up as companies limited by guarantee (CLG), are not required to publish their accounts but there will be some requirements should such clubs receive funding from the Sports Capital Programme (SCP). This will be further examined in **Chapter 10**. Sample financial statements can be viewed at **Appendix 14**;
- **Club Handbook:** The importance of integrated communication in sports clubs cannot be overstated. The deficit in communication is often most obvious when somebody who has just joined such an organisation is left to find out whatever they can by checking the website, notice boards, asking questions, etc. One could spend months in some clubs before getting to grips with their *modus operandi* – this hardly conveys the impression of the "welcoming and inclusive club". This scenario can be avoided by having a club handbook, which need not be a cumbersome tome but could be a

6. Governance

simple directory that would anticipate the usual questions, act as an ongoing reference point and make the newcomer feel at home. A club handbook can take many forms – a suggested template is attached at **Appendix 15**.

7. ORGANISATIONAL STRATEGY

Tactics without strategy is the noise before defeat.

(Sun Tzu, *The Art of War*)

We can wonder at how some sports clubs, often in the same code and competing at similar levels, can differ so much in terms of facilities, teams, gender balance, general approach and attitude. The answer is that all clubs are comprised of people – and the "right" people can mould themselves into synergetic units that not only understand the "why" of matters but can make the subsequent "how" happen. Other clubs often fail to find that combination – but it's not fatal because the personnel in any given scenario (beware of situations where committee members hang on too long!) will change and such change can spark a totally different dynamic.

Clubs require the proper level of management in order to satisfy the current needs of their members – but in order to envisage and satisfy, the future needs of members, strategic thinking is required.

7.1   The Need for Vision & Strategy

Sports clubs often can proceed at a tactical level, with solid committees providing sound leadership – but hard graft in terms of fundraising and facilities does not always provide optimum solutions to club development. There are numerous examples of clubs which, having made huge efforts to create better conditions, find that there is no space remaining for that practice pitch or other addition – that club, having spent significant funds, now finds itself limited by its current boundaries and is unable to attain its full potential. Such an eventuality could have been avoided if that club had the element of "vision".

Vision is the start-point for any club that intends to achieve a future that all of the membership can be proud of, can buy into and can work towards.

There are some interacting elements that need to work here – the *vision*, to be fully visible to the membership, has to be articulated by a *leader* who has the ability to draw the picture of the future, who can *persuade* the membership that this is *their future* and who can convince the key stakeholders that they should actively work towards this future.

What is afoot here is *strategic thinking* – convincing those concerned of the *why* (and fighting off the "sure, isn't it grand" brigade) and then teasing out the *how* so that all concerned understand the nature of the tasks involved and, most importantly, how projects will be funded. The difference between clubs, as alluded to earlier, usually boils down to *strategy*.

Strategy can be easily misunderstood. A long list of "things to do", often called "objectives", is not a strategy. A good strategy defines a critical challenge. Then, it builds a bridge between that challenge and action. A strategy contains three elements:

- A **diagnosis** that defines the nature of the challenge – this can simplify seeming complexity. A problem statement could also address this (what is the biggest problem facing this club?);
- A **guiding policy** for dealing with the challenge – an overall approach to overcome obstacles. Having identified the problem(careful here!), the club decides how to find the solution;
- A set of **coherent actions** that are designed to carry out the guiding policy. Knowing the solution, setting out a plan to achieve the solution.

A sports club contemplating the formulation of a strategy should tackle the task using a coherent methodology. Better conditions for strategy formulation will exist if some member (*leader*) or members (*leadership group*) come to the conclusion that "something needs to be done" (as against "let's come up with a strategy"). This is known as the "trigger".

There are prerequisites here – the club must have a recognisable ethos or set of values and, of course, it must have an agreed purpose. The leadership element, fully understanding the values and purpose of the organisation, then can create the vision for the organisation. **Figure 8** shows the importance of the leadership / values / purpose combination.

The next step is vital. The **vision** as constructed must be articulated in a manner that makes it both achievable and attractive to the body of membership. Communication, a critical tool often misused by clubs, must be deftly managed here if the picture of the future is to be sold to the membership body. This whole process is greatly facilitated by having a *mission statement*. The best version of this is the military version: **Who, What, When, Where and Why**. The *How* will be undertaken by the set of coherent actions as mentioned above.

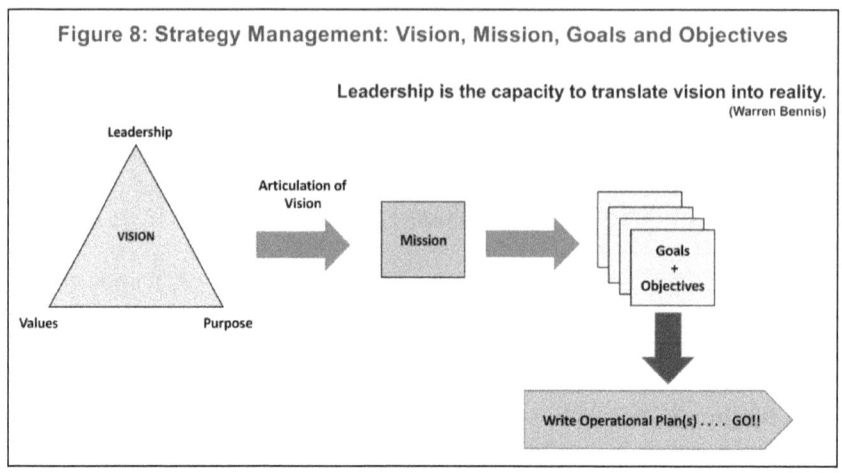

Source: Corporate Strategy for Irish Companies, G. Gallagher, 2009.

The *mission* for the club is a derivative of the *vision* but it hardens that future picture into a more honed process. The mission then can be moved towards reality by creating *goals* for the club. Care is needed here – the organisation that boasts it has "10 or 12 goals" is simply confused. The club that comes up with two or three goals has done the *diagnosis* properly.

You may cry "but how do we get everything done with only three goals?" This is achieved by simply breaking down the few goals into objectives – a goal could have any number of related objectives.

In this way, the original *vision* is now being edged towards actionable tasks. Those tasks can then be brought to life through the creation of simple operational plans – one objective or group of objectives could become operational through a simple plan that indicates the task, the timeline, the person or committee responsible, review dates, closure date, etc.

We have now come from the casting of a picture to having operational tasks being divided between particular persons or sub-committees. It would be useful, indeed imperative, for any club embarking on strategy formulation, to focus on the core function of strategy as shown in **Figure 9**.

Be careful with the question "where are we now?" – the answer to it may not be that simple! One good way to address that question is to complete a comprehensive PESTLE (PESTEL) Analysis and / or SWOT Analysis (see **Appendix 16**). This is an important first step, so seek assistance if not familiar with this process.

7. Organisational Strategy

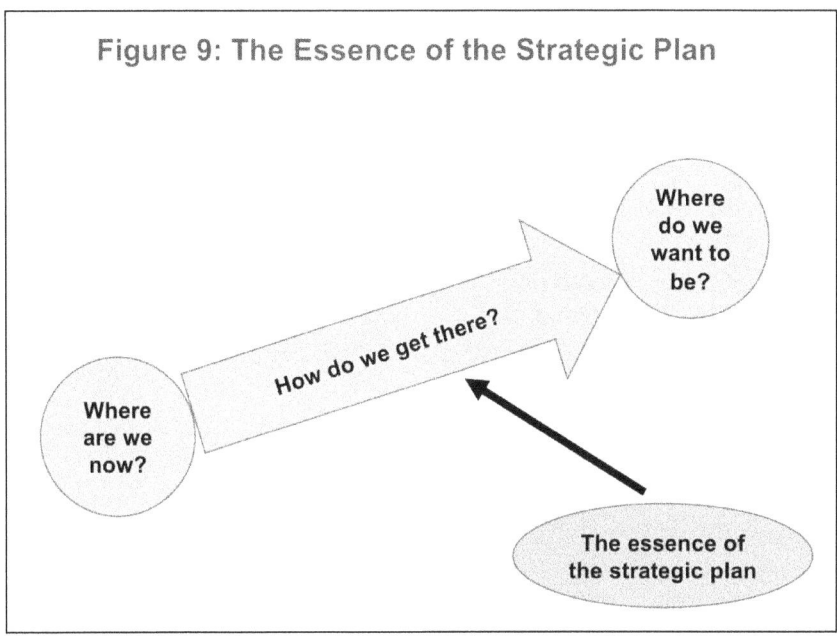

Figure 9: The Essence of the Strategic Plan

The *how* involves the planning, the work, the fundraising and, most importantly, the commitment. There are four main phases to be negotiated here, as shown in **Figure 10**.

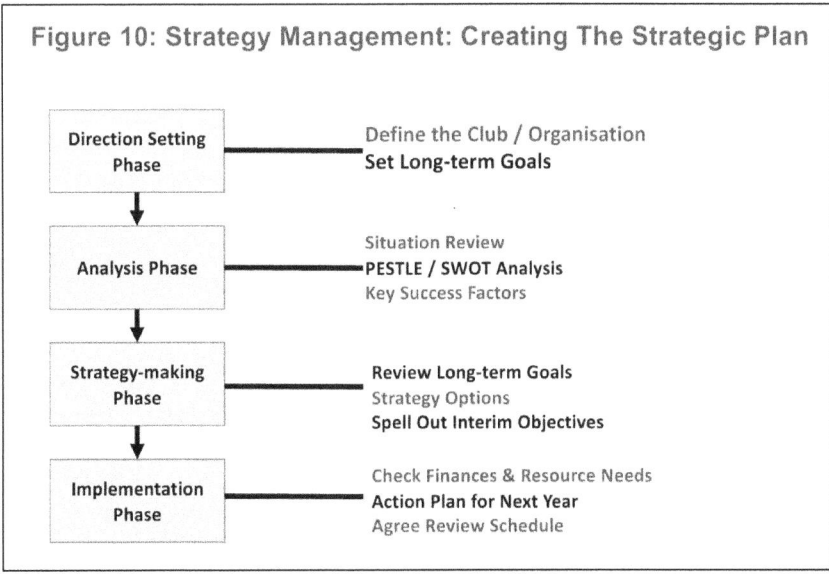

Figure 10: Strategy Management: Creating The Strategic Plan

There are many advantages to having a strategic plan:
- It sets the organisation on a definite path for the following three to five years;
- It gives a sense of direction and a feeling of ownership of their future to the membership;
- It prioritises various projects and channels fundraising efforts into an all-club mode;
- It provides an agreed pathway that overrides changes of committees and personnel;
- It can accommodate smaller projects, providing they do not contravene the strategic plan;
- It can prevent (sometimes costly) "solo runs" by particular elements within the organisation;
- It caters for the ongoing monitoring and evaluation of developments within the organisation.

The above points should not confer the impression that a strategic plan is some rigid intervention that binds the organisation to an ongoing future burden – a strategic plan can be changed at an AGM or EGM to meet changing circumstances.

The creation of a strategic plan for a club is usually triggered by a particular event, the realisation by a committee that the organisation has significant needs or by the emergence of a leader who articulates what needs to be done to drive the organisation forward. Care is needed here and some cautious steps are required just to get to the start-line:
- The "concept" or raw idea needs to be fully distilled before it is presented to any committee or interest group – placing a "woolly" idea on the table often results in misunderstandings, encourages the nay-sayers and discourages the source of the original idea;
- The person or persons putting forward ideas for development can be a factor – some clubs can be dominated by strong personalities who often dismiss the concerns of others – these concerns will be manifested later by a lack of support in areas such as fundraising, etc. A strategic plan needs buy-in across the club;
- The person or persons behind the idea usually end up in control of the project so that person or persons must be capable of organising the required resources – those who throw ideas on committee tables but who are not prepared to convert ideas into reality will never get any traction. A basic concept or idea always can be "tested" through conversations with members in different areas of the club;

7. Organisational Strategy

- If the General Committee is sufficiently persuaded by a well-articulated proposal, then the seeds of a strategy are sown. The Committee should then authorise the proposer to form a project team with the purpose of creating a strategic plan for the club. This delegation is important – a large General Committee undertaking such a task is a recipe for much discussion and no action. So, a Strategy Project Team (SPT) that reports frequently to the General Committee, should set about the task of creating a strategic plan.

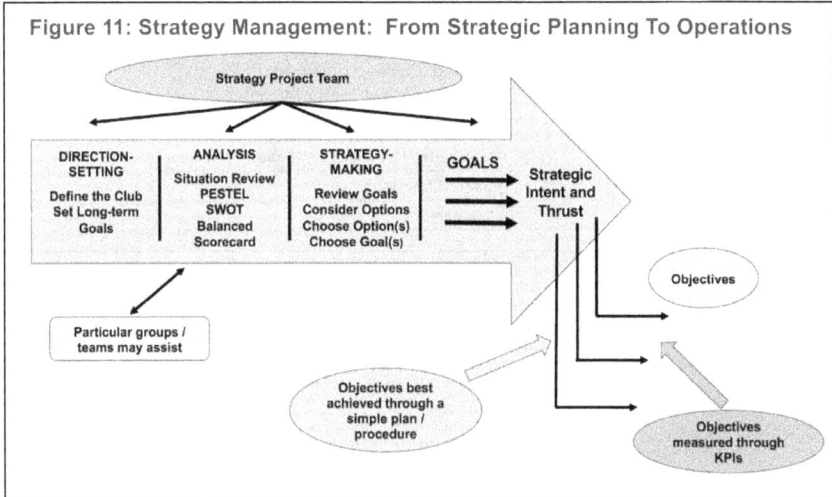

Figure 11: Strategy Management: From Strategic Planning To Operations

The route to be taken by the SPT, as illustrated in **Figure 11**, has definite phases, all of which have to be handled carefully.

The leader of the SPT, most likely the proposer of the original idea or concept needs to be many things – a good communicator, a persuader, a detailed administrator, a taskmaster, a politician and a worker! Clubs can become very political, so those who stick their heads above the parapet need to be strong, purposeful individuals. But this can be seen from different angles – the clubs that do not have major challenges facing them are the ones that descend into wasteful bickering. A goal that requires hard work and significant fundraising focuses minds and minimises internal politics.

That said, when the SPT finalises its strategic plan, it should present it to the General Committee. It may be useful to conduct a full PowerPoint presentation, having issued briefing documents to the members of the committee in advance. If the strategic plan is accepted, the objectives (derived from the goals) can then be actioned through simple operational plans, as shown in **Figure 12.**

Figure 12: Strategy Management: Operational Plan Template(s)

Strategic Objective	To grow under-age membership at the ABC [Sport] Club.
Goals	To increase registered under-age players by 25 before the start of the Christmas holidays.
Initiatives	Visit local secondary schools with Christmas school holiday promotional brochure for teachers and children. Local radio advertising for Open Day and Christmas school holiday promotion.
Performance Indicators	Promotional brochure produced. Radio advertising placed. Open Day held at club. Under-age players increased by 25 players.
Budget	€X,000.
Timeline	Brochure produced – 1 October. All local schools visited – 1 November. Radio advertising placed – 25 November. Open Day hosted – 1 December. New members recruited – 15 December.
Responsibility	General Manager.
Progress	In progress.

Suggested templates for a strategic plan and operational plans are attached in **Appendix 16**.

8. LEADERSHIP & MANAGEMENT

The spirit of an organisation is created from the top.

(Peter Drucker)

It's not a question of *either* leadership *or* management. All good clubs reflect strengths in both areas – and they are separate areas. The accepted wisdom on this topic is that management is "doing things right", while leadership is "doing the right thing". If only we could know what the "right thing" is! Having a solid, well-considered strategic plan ensures that a sports club is as close to the "right thing" as is humanly possible at any given point in time.

It is also proposed that management is "dealing with complexity", while leadership "deals with change". While this is a tidy appraisal of the difference between both, it must be accepted that:

- Clubs are populated by humans with all their frailties; and
- There are political agendas at play in most cases.

So it may often be the case that those who work hard for their clubs can be taken for granted, while those who want to drive matters forward are often accused of "following an agenda".

Sports clubs can be difficult places, so those who want to improve their club need to be strong characters who can be persuasive and can build coalitions. Various unfolding circumstances often can prompt the emergence of leaders. Leadership can take time to have an effect because of the lag between a concept and actions resulting in outputs – in the meantime, the club has to be managed.

The basis for good management is found in a proactive Chairperson / Secretary relationship, a coordinated General Committee and committed volunteers in critical areas such as fundraising, coaching, under-age development, etc. When these different levels of volunteers can see the same organisational picture and avoid sectional interests, then that club can go as far as it can see. But, in pursuing its objectives, the club has to be managed.

There are five elements:

- **Planning** involves making solid decisions about what needs to be done, the sequence and timeline for taking actions to get those things done, the allocation of resources to support the decisions taken, the reduction of uncertainty about the future and the avoidance of impulsive and arbitrary decisions. Plans should be simple and easily understood so that the membership can support them. Such plans should be consistent, but also be flexible enough to meet the demands of dynamic club systems;
- **Organising** is the means to get things done in an efficient manner. Members of clubs become deflated quickly if a sense of disorganisation emerges. Organising involves the identification and classification of the required activities, the grouping of such activities so as to attain objectives and the assignment of each grouping of activities to an individual who has been given the authority and means of coordination to get the job done;
- **Staffing** in a club means, mostly, the selection of volunteers who are willing to take on a share of the tasks required to get a project completed. The project leader here must endeavour to maintain an enjoyable environment to ensure that volunteers can get satisfaction from their collaboration while putting in a consistently enthusiastic effort;
- **Directing** is necessary to avoid a breakout of "headless chicken" syndrome – it involves the issuing of instructions and schedules so that those carrying out the tasks become comfortable in understanding the requirement. It also involves good, ongoing communication so that there is full visibility of the objectives. Good decision-making at various points is necessary so that any deviation from the objectives is avoided;
- **Controlling** can cause some irritation if not properly exercised – this is especially pertinent in clubs where most contributions are freely given. Enthusiasm is a gift that most clubs appreciate but there must be an element of control in all events or chaos will ensue. Control can be exercised through good communication, fully explaining the standards to be achieved and ongoing monitoring so that deviations can be corrected.

Only those who will risk going too far can possibly find out how far one can go.

(TS Eliot)

8. Leadership & Management

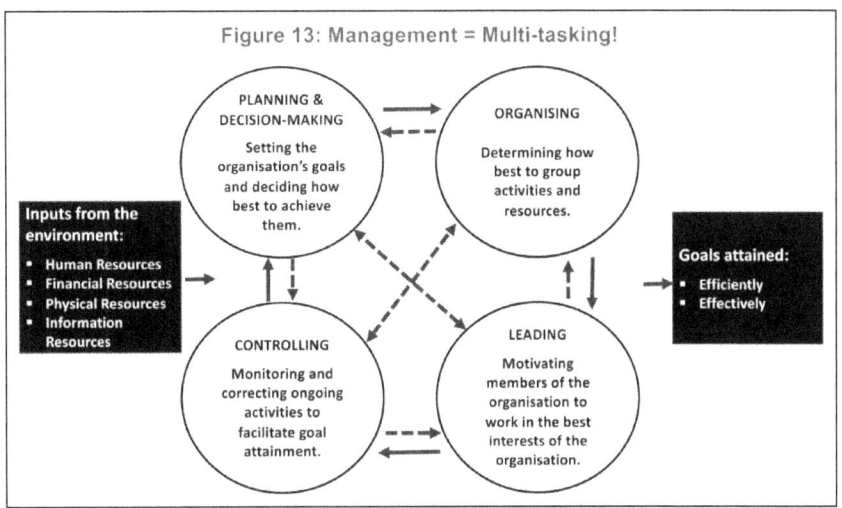

Figure 13: Management = Multi-tasking!

We often think of leaders and entrepreneurs as "risk takers" but that is to misunderstand them. They are *not* risk takers – they try to define the risk and to minimise it as much as possible. This is pertinent to clubs because all such entities throw up those who are willing and able to lead – to take on responsibilities for the benefit of their club.

Willingness to lead in a club requires an ability to be patient, to play the long game, to convince those whose world view sees no reason to move forward, to articulate ideas and to persuade various elements to expand or exit from their comfort zones. Leadership here has to bear in mind that all involved are volunteers and are well disposed towards their club – so one has to proceed gently so as not to alienate any sections. There are times, of course, when some tough talking has to be done and that comes naturally to the leader who instinctively knows when a forceful argument has to be made.

But a leader in a voluntary club setting has to understand *risk* – not just monetary risk, which can become problematic if hard-won funding is misspent or does not produce expected outcomes, but also *perceived risk* – why should the membership trust somebody selling an idea? What is to stop a club officer, who is a volunteer, from walking away from a project that has gone wrong and has created unforeseen debt? Nothing, really. But it usually does not unfold in that manner – the leader in a club does not just materialise in a moment and take the club on some mystery tour – that leader will have created a track record through holding office, involvement in various fundraising projects and will have shown a willingness to put in the effort and to support others in their endeavours. So, trust in that person has been built over a period.

There are many types of leadership such as *trait leadership, situational leadership,* etc. – the model most seen in voluntary organisations is probably that of *transformational leadership*. This is logical as most organisations produce people who are not content with the *status quo* and who want more for themselves, their fellow members and future members. This need to improve has now intensified as there is fierce competition between various sports codes and voluntary organisations to acquire and retain members.

Leadership initiatives in clubs require a coordination of interactions if any event is to succeed. The three big factors at play here are:

- The leader;
- The proposed event to be organised; and
- The ongoing interactions between that leader and the "followers" – the club members who have been persuaded by the leader.

The current club environment has also to be considered.

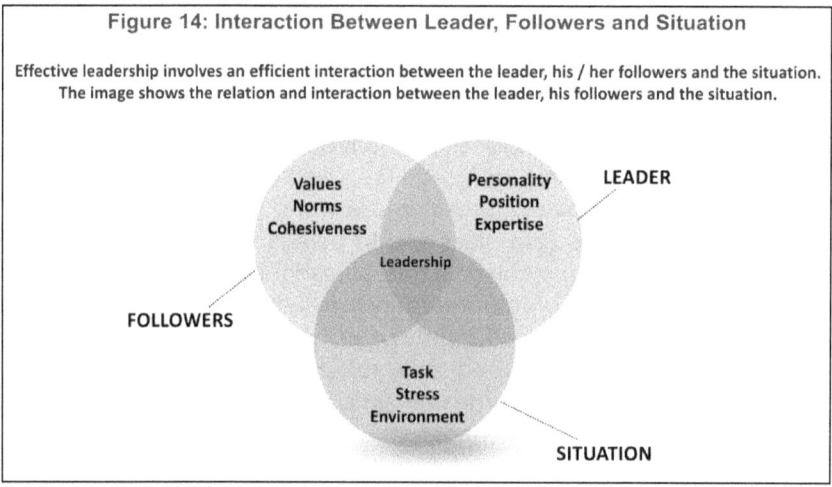

Figure 14: Interaction Between Leader, Followers and Situation

Effective leadership involves an efficient interaction between the leader, his / her followers and the situation. The image shows the relation and interaction between the leader, his followers and the situation.

Leadership in club situations need not rest on the shoulders of individuals – exchanges of ideas between particular members often creates the energy to move such ideas towards reality and then uses their collective commitment to get the job done. In these scenarios, it is advisable for such individuals or groups to initially go for a "small win" – in other words, take on some reasonably small project and complete it on time and within budget. This result then gives a strong signal to the organisation on the capabilities of this group. That group then will have the confidence and the backing to try something more ambitious. **Figure 14** illustrates the relationship between the leader and their understanding of their role, the norms that are accepted in the club and the task to be addressed in that particular environment.

The dynamics between this leadership group (soon to become a project team) and the General Committee are an important factor so the process could unfold thus:

- The leadership group should assemble its raw ideas into a coherent plan, or at least a set of manageable steps – all members need to be on the same page as to its intent;
- This group then signals its intentions to the General Committee and arranges for a presentation of the proposed idea – this need not be overly elaborate but it could include some documentation and, perhaps, a PowerPoint presentation – the General Committee needs to be fully appraised of what is being proposed;
- The General Committee then should carefully consider the proposal in the light of other activities in the organisation. If they are satisfied that this project should go ahead, then they should hand the project back to the project team. They should:
  - Resist the temptation to take over the project themselves – large committees do not have a good track record in managing projects – too much talk, too many counter-ideas, loose lines of responsibility, long control spans, prevarication, competing tasks, etc., etc.
  - Allow individuals and groups who are willing to create ideas to do just that rather than discouraging such initiatives by being seen to take over projects with potential.
- The project team, having received permission, now needs to complete a cohesive plan, allocate tasks within its group (recognising that the team members have various capabilities), assess the resources required and procure all possible support from various sections of the club. It would be advantageous if this (early win) initial project had revenue-raising potential in itself (for example, all-weather pitches that could provide a revenue stream for years to come) so that twofold objectives of adding facilities and acquiring revenue are achieved.

A material demonstration of leadership such as this can lift the whole organisation, confer a fresh confidence in its abilities and generate more constructive ideas. The development of voluntary entities is always driven from within and the extent of that development correlates to the quality of leadership to be found therein.

Those who think they have what it takes will put their hands up and will not easily be dissuaded from doing what they think is right for their club. Those leaders are recognised by three general traits – they:

- Go above and beyond;
- Have a great attitude;
- Play well with others.

9. MARKETING

Like it or not, the market's perception becomes your reality.

(Howard Mann, Actor)

Whether it is considered as a core club activity, marketing is an essential pursuit for *all* clubs because the competition for local, regional and national resources is intense and all advantages are hard-won. Most clubs recognise this but do not always positively react to this imperative. They want to be recognised, to be part of the local landscape but often fail to appreciate that clever, ongoing promotion is essential to achieving this.

Marketing in a club environment requires continued coordination across several areas which include the club website, active use of various social media platforms, a really good public relations officer (PRO) who takes the time to build relationships with local radio, newspapers, county and provincial officials and sponsors.

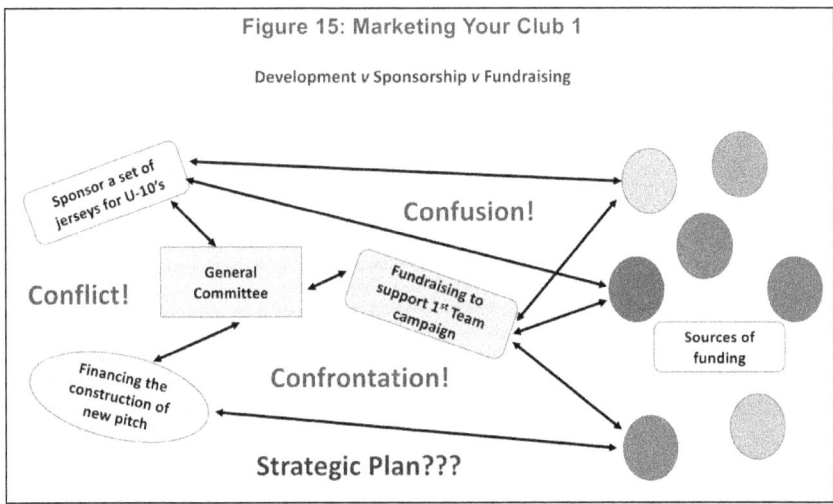

Figure 15 should be familiar to many clubs – there is no coordination between the various sections of the club, which all engage in their own

pursuits. The diagram shows one prospective source of funding being approached by both the First Team management and the pitch-building committee – this scattergun approach can result in neither party getting anything!

Marketing can be defined as: "human activity directed at satisfying *needs and wants* through exchange processes" (Philip Kotler, *Marketing Management*, 1976). It is important for the sports club to understand that "needs and wants" exist on both sides so that club should realise how it will satisfy the needs and wants of those individuals or businesses who are being targeted. "What can we give to the sponsor in return for their generosity?" is a most common question in clubs – and one that often is not thought through properly. In some cases, fortunately, the sponsor will not want anything in return but, in most cases, a *quid pro quo* is the norm.

9.1 The Marketing Mix

It is probably best, in any marketing approach, to use the *marketing mix* to evaluate the club and to construct a marketing strategy on that basis.

The marketing mix is based on four pillars (the 4Ps):

- **Product:** Product, in many cases, can be a service and not a physical offering so a club has options here – both the facilities and the activities that are made possible by such facilities can be seen as a package and be "sold" as such. Clubs with synthetic pitches, lighting, gyms and gender-specific dressing rooms obviously have a lot to promote but all clubs must package their assets into an attractive option;

- **Place:** Many sports clubs do not own their premises but the *place* can still be marketed because it's not just about the physical location – it's very much about the *people* who, after all, constitute the essence of the club. Additionally, the "4 Ps" should not be separated but should always be seen as a part of the whole – so, even though the local swimming club does not own the municipal pool, it can market what it does, the successes it has achieved, etc;

- **Price:** Price here can be viewed from either side – the price for its members to join the club and the "price" the prospective sponsor is expected to pay for the privilege of supporting the club. Sports clubs seek sponsors of various types to purchase jerseys, help construct a pitch, etc. - so the price can vary to meet particular circumstances;

- **Promotion:** The other three Ps will not bear fruit unless the fourth P is fully implemented. Good promotion is about projecting the best possible aspects of the club into the local community or whatever segment of the market is selected. This is where *product* and *brand*

9. Marketing

need to be understood – the club and all it achieves can be moulded into a *brand* – not just to attract new members but also to convince potential sponsors that their financial support is worthwhile.

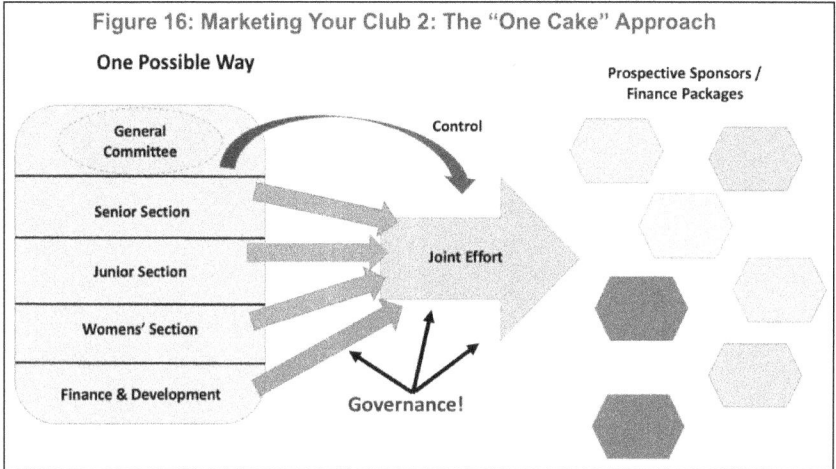

Figure 16 suggests an approach that all clubs might consider: the club funding is seen as one "cake" to be eaten by all sections – but the making of the cake is also the responsibility of all sections.

So, under the direction of the General Committee, all marketing targets are agreed on a club-wide basis and the detailed approach also is agreed. All sections must work towards fundraising and marketing and all resultant funds should go into a club pot – that pot to be divided among the various sections of the club based on the decisions of the General Committee.

Marketing and fundraising must be targeted and controlled if the club is to take full advantage of its reputation and standing in the local community. Individual sections in some clubs see themselves as almost independent entities and so they compete for sponsorship. This is a mistake – it sows confusion, it distorts the target market, and it can create resentment and division among those sections. The General Committee should always promote the "one club" strategy so that marketing is conducted through one channel and ensure that all resultant benefits are divided equitably.

The notion of having a marketing plan may be scoffed at in some organisations which would rather raise funds in an *ad hoc* manner. This is a short-sighted strategy, particularly if the organisation is a strong one with good membership. Marketing takes the long-term view and sports clubs that can think strategically will realise the value of such action.

A marketing plan need not be the complex idea beloved of commercial giants – it can be scaled down to suit the essentials of a sports club. A suggested template for a marketing plan is attached in **Appendix 17.**

10. FUNDRAISING & FINANCE

If you want a guarantee, buy a toaster.

(Clint Eastwood)

There is certainly no guarantee that any fundraising project organised by a club will result in the envisaged outputs – stories abound of disastrous efforts in this area. Fundraising, as any active club member knows, is hard work, which needs focus and commitment. Sports clubs that are working under pressure towards financial targets often have a healthier outlook than clubs that have all the facilities and are in cruise mode. However, clubs embarking on fundraising projects, particularly those involving significant amounts of finance, should be aware of some common areas of concern:

- There is often not enough communication surrounding the project, so some sections of the club are not included – it is imperative that the whole organisation fully understands the objectives involved, how the project will evolve, etc;
- Tensions can arise between those who organise all the fundraising efforts and those who will eventually decide how such funding will be spent *("we're raising all the money and now they're spending it irresponsibly")*. The General Committee should not cede control or leadership in such situations – fundraising sub-committees should not be allowed to become "little republics" that insist on conducting matters on their terms only. Detailed discussions resulting in a clear understanding by all those involved are essential to avoid any possible conflict;
- Fundraising efforts by sections within the club require close oversight by the General Committee so that all financing objectives are aligned and that one such effort does not impinge on another;
- Fundraising targets will need to be coordinated – approaches to prospective benefactors by different sections of a club do not reflect well on that club and may result in no benefit being accrued. Approaches need to be smart and should not "spoil" the club's

perceived market – if a club needs to raise €5,000, then its first option is to try to raise it in one location. In many such cases, where €5,000 is needed, 100 people may be asked to donate €50 – fine, but, if the €5,000 is raised from one source, then the club still retains a "market" of 99 other people who can be approached for something else;
- It must be abundantly clear from the outset how finance raised by a sports club is to be spent – there can be no ambiguity here – any attempt by a General Committee to change the purpose of a fundraising project when the money has been raised will result in serious conflict – there are many instances where clubs have split up over such decisions;
- Sports clubs that involve themselves in development projects must act, and be seen to act, as "one club for everybody" – the club must be seen as a cake to be enjoyed by all members. This is particularly important in multi-sport clubs where, to ensure total support, all funds raised must be distributed in a visible and ethical fashion. One way to ensure this is through a clear club strategy where all members can see the planned projects and understand that all facilities will receive financial support in their turn. This is a reminder of the importance of having capable officers in charge of the club at all times – a couple of years without strong leadership can destabilise any club, damage its ethos, create uncertainty and hinder future progress;
- It is important to have a fundraising strategy within the club's strategy – and to have a "fundraising calendar" for each year that outlines the major events to be planned, which areas will benefit from various efforts and the particular personnel to be involved in different projects. This calendar should also provide a "mix" of fundraising events – an event that requires the selling of a large quantity of tickets should not be followed by a similar event – selling tickets is not a popular task!
- All fundraising efforts should be evaluated in terms of the finance raised in relation to the resources and effort involved – using Pareto Analysis (the 80 / 20 rule). Such honest evaluation may be disheartening at times but fundraising events that do not produce results should be discarded;
- Some events, such as golf classics, become identified with a club and become a welcome annual fixture – the continuity also allows the club the develop an expertise in the event and to improve its content on an ongoing basis. If it works, and makes money, keep doing it!

10. Fundraising & Finance

- That said, a club should continue to investigate fundraising events and should be prepared to embark on something new from time to time. A new event may require different expertise and different people but that is healthy – in many cases, those who have proven ability in the area of fundraising are often left to their own devices and in time can become tired and disenchanted – fundraisers always need cooperation and support;

As said previously, fundraising and financing in a club environment can raise hackles if not carefully managed and communicated openly. It is perceived in many large rugby and GAA clubs that the main focus of funding is to support the club's first team and the rest of the organisation gets the "crumbs from the table". Proving that this is or is not the case is the responsibility of the General Committee, which must oversee the club in an even-handed manner. Care must be taken not to alienate those who work hard in the fundraising area.

There are of course other means of raising finance – most NGBs have schemes to support clubs, whether they be loans on favourable long-term terms or grants that can be accessed if the club can satisfy particular criteria. Funds can also be accessed through Sport Ireland, Local Authorities, LSPs, etc. Research by the club can quickly uncover what is available.

10.1 Sports Capital Programme

Development programmes in clubs can benefit significantly by acquiring funding from the SCP, which is operated by the Department of Transport, Tourism & Sport. Applying for such funding requires quite an amount of preparation and work so one should read into the detail of the SCP or other programme before making any preparations.

A few points in relation to the SCP:

- Applications usually require ancillary documentation, perhaps planning permission, etc. so there can be a reasonably long lead-in time. One may have to engage with the club's solicitor (title deeds, etc.) so time has to be devoted to this. Start early!
- The person responsible for the application should be the one to register on the system called "OSCAR" (Online Sports Capital Register) because the system is not flexible enough to allow multiple persons to access it;
- The person making the application should be a good administrator with a sharp eye for detail.

- Ensure that all the requirements, such as the need to show that the club has a percentage of the required sum in a separate bank account, are fully understood;
- Most importantly, and regardless of what the Department or the Minister might say, there is a political element to this exercise – so ensure that the club has political support for its application. Don't be shy here – every other applicant will be doing it!

11. OPERATIONS & ADMINISTRATION

No matter how expert you may be, a well-designed checklist can improve outcomes.

(Steven Levitt, *Freakonomics*)

The structure of a sports club has a direct impact on the quality of its administration and *vice versa*. Such structures remain static unless they are administered fully and administration cannot be effective unless there are proper structures in place.

Clubs come in all shapes and sizes and therefore have different approaches in this regard. For example, some clubs have formal office premises while, in many cases, there is no formal structure with club officers retaining documentation in their own homes. There should be agreed procedures in place to cater for such different approaches.

There are many clubs operating at present that have very poor governance, have little appreciation of what is required to achieve optimum efficiency and which are, in some instances, in breach of legislative requirements. Clubs that fail to fully assess their operations and to implement proper processes and procedures are not only falling short on the original objectives for that club but are failing the members who have a right to be part of any entity that fully serves their aspirations.

Some suggestions here in relation to administration:

- There should be **job descriptions** to fit all the roles in the club – to clarify what is required of each officer, establish distinct spans of control and prohibit any squabbles as to responsibilities;
- If there is an **office**, then access to it and its contents should be restricted so that the principle of confidentiality is preserved;
- Care is needed if there is no office and club documentation is retained in the homes of officers – it is strongly recommended that, in such cases, the club should issue the Secretary, and perhaps the Chairperson, with club laptops and mobile phones. Such devices, and the materials gathered on them, remain the property of the club. This arrangement should be documented and signed off so that there is no ambiguity – there have been many cases where a

- club's Secretary has had a dispute with their club and has refused to hand over documentation and records;
- If a sports club employs a person in any capacity, then the club must supply that employee with a contract of **employment** (CoE) within two months of commencement. Clubs should exercise care here – when such clubs become employers they become answerable to employment law, of which there is an abundance in this country. The situation can become even more complex if the club employs somebody who is already a member of that organisation – that person now has two roles which could conflict each other in particular circumstances. This arrangement has thrown up some awkward situations in the past so clubs should reflect carefully before allowing such an arrangement to arise;
- The operation and administration of **club insurance** should be strictly controlled – the members constitute the club – so, in normal circumstances, a club member cannot sue the club because he or she *is the club* – one cannot sue oneself. Therefore, players or members who have not paid their membership (a common condition!) *are not members* and should *never* be allowed to train, play or use the club facilities because, if they are injured, they will be free to sue the club. Many clubs fail to observe this measure and some have paid dearly for this oversight;
- Clubs must observe, and be seen to observe, their own **rules**. Such rules and procedures have been set up for a purpose and to allow such regulations to be circumvented in any way is to send the wrong signal to members. Other rules can be laid down by sports bodies at a county, competition or provincial level so such rules obtain both within the club and in the operating context of that club. In such context, "Under-16" must mean literally that – clubs who seek to bend rules in such situations are not just creating a short-term impression that "anything goes" but are also contributing in the long term to the creation of a club culture that will damage the club ethos. Do you want to be a member of a club with this attitude?
- **Operational and administrative procedures** should be set up by every club so that they are prepared for various contingencies. Clubs are too often thrown into confusion by some incident, often of a disciplinary nature, that catches the club management off-guard. Having such procedures in place allows the club to react to incidents in a calm, considered manner. There are people in every club who are good at this type of procedural documentation – a regular review of all club documentation is a worthwhile endeavour;

- **Payments** of any kind to any club member, if such has to be done, must be conducted on the basis of agreed, documented procedures. There are circumstances whereby players may be paid an allowance to travel to their club for training – all of these arrangements are fine if they are properly set up and agreed by the General Committee and are fully documented. Other situations whereby "nixers" are paid to club members for undertaking particular activities are fraught with danger and should be avoided;
- **Clubs with bars** assume extra responsibilities. In such cases, a Bar Chairperson should be appointed by the General Committee. This appointment requires a job description and the bar operation should be covered by a detailed procedure that covers opening times, staff control, stock management, cash management, etc. Club bars, in addition to their own internal rules, are governed by the current licencing laws;
- **Sports kit, leisure wear and merchandising** are well-organised in many clubs and can become significant revenue streams. This again has to be controlled, either through the office or by an appointed person. All club kit and gear should be purchased through a single channel if possible and sales of such kit, including online sales, must be strictly accounted for. Systems whereby members or parents / guardians of under-age members can pay for kit by instalments in advance can be set up but extending credit should be avoided;
- **Match tickets** can become a source of conflict unless a clear and equitable system is set up for the benefit of members. Tickets can be distributed on the basis of work done for the club, *via* a draw system, etc. as long as it is perceived as fair. International match tickets are used by some clubs as a source of revenue – a practice that goes against the grain and should be discouraged. The sale of match tickets should be strongly controlled by the General Committee, up to the point of governing the practice through the club Constitution;
- **Ordering goods and services**, without the prior permission of the General Committee, is a practice that, unfortunately, is alive and well and is the bane of all Treasurers. When committees are faced with bills for items that were not authorised, that committee and its treasurer are placed in an unenviable position – taking a stand and refusing to pay would put an end to such activity and set an example for all members. This again highlights the fact that strong committees and solid officers can prevent a lot of mismanagement.

One could discuss operations and administration *ad nauseam* – it is probably better to ask: what would the best club do?

The best club would have a deep understanding of what is its *raison d'être*, would have a strategy for the optimum development of the club and would chase its objectives while acting with integrity in all matters.

Most clubs need people who can lead regardless of the conditions. Every club, at some point, may find itself in choppy waters – good leadership will anticipate the storm and will weather it. One of the basics of military training is to instil the troops with trust in their officers – the same principle will serve the sports club. The General Committee and its officers must earn the trust of the members. Achieve that much and it will be relatively plain sailing thereafter.

Figure 17 is offered as an *aide memoire* for those involved in club operations. Remember the two main planks: the operation itself and the administration of that operation – both are equally important.

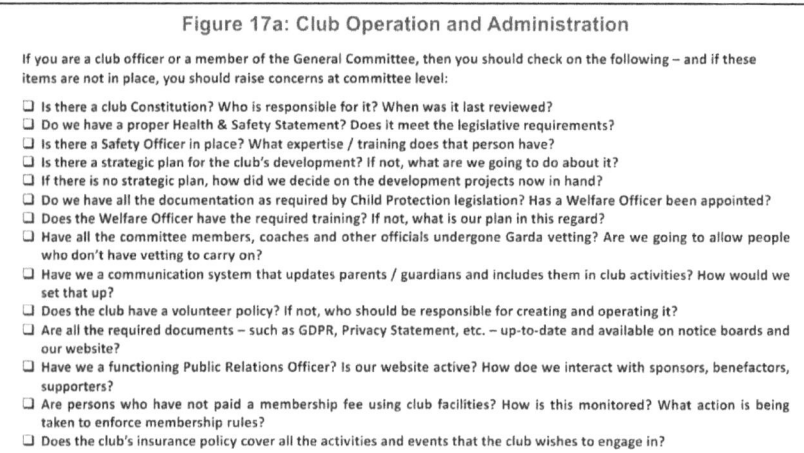

Figure 17a: Club Operation and Administration

If you are a club officer or a member of the General Committee, then you should check on the following – and if these items are not in place, you should raise concerns at committee level:

- Is there a club Constitution? Who is responsible for it? When was it last reviewed?
- Do we have a proper Health & Safety Statement? Does it meet the legislative requirements?
- Is there a Safety Officer in place? What expertise / training does that person have?
- Is there a strategic plan for the club's development? If not, what are we going to do about it?
- If there is no strategic plan, how did we decide on the development projects now in hand?
- Do we have all the documentation as required by Child Protection legislation? Has a Welfare Officer been appointed?
- Does the Welfare Officer have the required training? If not, what is our plan in this regard?
- Have all the committee members, coaches and other officials undergone Garda vetting? Are we going to allow people who don't have vetting to carry on?
- Have we a communication system that updates parents / guardians and includes them in club activities? How would we set that up?
- Does the club have a volunteer policy? If not, who should be responsible for creating and operating it?
- Are all the required documents – such as GDPR, Privacy Statement, etc. – up-to-date and available on notice boards and our website?
- Have we a functioning Public Relations Officer? Is our website active? How doe we interact with sponsors, benefactors, supporters?
- Are persons who have not paid a membership fee using club facilities? How is this monitored? What action is being taken to enforce membership rules?
- Does the club's insurance policy cover all the activities and events that the club wishes to engage in?

11. Operations & Administration

Figure 17b: Club Operation and Administration

- ❏ Are minutes of meetings being read at meetings or "taken as read"? The Secretary should accurately *record* the minutes and not *interpret* what is said.
- ❏ Are club matters being discussed and actioned "off-table" by members of the General Committee and not being referred to at committee meetings?
- ❏ How are documented minutes handled? Are they recorded on devices not in the ownership of the club? What system is in place to safeguard minutes?
- ❏ Are there instances where correspondence is received by the club and responded to (or not responded to) without being aired at committee meetings?
- ❏ Is there satisfactory control of financial matters generally? Is there a purchase order system in place? If not, how is purchasing controlled? What happens if the club is billed for a purchased item that it did not authorise?
- ❏ What is the nature of the relationships between the General Committee and sub-committees? Do the sub-committees raise funds in their own right? How does the Club Treasurer control this?
- ❏ Is there a coordinated plan to support fundraising? How are prospective sponsors targeted and how are approaches controlled? If there is no plan, what should be done?
- ❏ Are the keys to the club premises in general, or particular parts of the club, properly controlled or is there general access? Do particular persons control keys and not allow access to club officials to particular areas?
- ❏ If the club employs persons such as coaches, grounds-people, etc., do such staff have contracts of employment? Is there a policy on employing people who are already club members?
- ❏ Are the terms of service of club officers as specified in the club's Constitution being observed? What should be the response if there are efforts being made to circumvent this?
- ❏ Does the club operate a shop of any kind, to sell club merchandise or refreshments? How is this controlled? Who orders stock? Are accounts maintained or is it a loose cash system?

Figure 17c: Club Operation and Administration

- ❏ Is the attendance at committee meetings generally good? Do some committee members attend only infrequently? Are there vacancies on the General Committee? If so, are such vacancies being filled? How often does the general membership of the committee change? Is the AGM generally well attended? Is there a perception that the General Committee is a closed shop? Is there ever any attempt to get expertise, whether in the club or from outside, onto the General Committee? Are issues such as the above being addressed?
- ❏ Do some volunteers in the club get paid in any way for tasks performed? Is there a blind eye turned to this? Is there a policy governing this? Do some people receive payment for using their own mobile phones?
- ❏ How is under-age transport for away games managed? Do parents / guardians drive or are buses hired? Is there a policy on this?
- ❏ Is there a programme to develop coaches internally or are coaches just hired in? What is the club attitude to this?
- ❏ Is a training / playing expenses budget for senior teams agreed in advance? Are medical expenses in respect of playing injuries controlled or just paid without question?
- ❏ Are new ideas welcomed at committee level or is there a general resistance to change? How long is it since a new idea was actioned or since a sub-committee tackled a development project of any kind?
- ❏ Are the senior sections and under-age sections acting like separate domains or does the General Committee strive to maintain a "one club" environment? Are discussions held on this topic?
- ❏ Is there any kind of filing system to retain and maintain the club's documents that accumulate over the years? Where are such documents? Is responsibility for this given to a particular person?
- ❏ Are there occasions when club equipment (gym equipment, sets of jerseys, laptops, projectors, etc.) is removed from the club premises for any reason? What control measures are in place? What is club policy on this?
- ❏ Are queries from any committee member fully considered or is this kind of approach discouraged?

12. PLANNING EVENTS

It's not the plan that counts, it's the planning.

(Gen. D. Eisenhower)

Most sports clubs have people within their ranks who are natural organisers – so it's surprising that many clubs fail to find the talent that lies within their own ranks. Any event, to produce successful outputs, requires an organiser who understands exactly what is to be achieved, who can persuade others as to what must be achieved, who understands the resources and investment required and who can put all the necessary pieces together in a timeline that will achieve the desired results.

Let us differentiate here between projects and events:

- A project could involve the building of a club's all-weather pitch over a two-year time span;
- An event, or series of events, could be planned to raise finance towards that pitch project.

While these two sets of activities are related, they need people with different skill-sets, with different objectives and with alternative operational approaches.

12.1 The Project Leader

The person taking charge of an event needs to have a solid appreciation of the "big picture" so that he or she can visualise the event timeline from start to finish and anticipate any possible problems. Enthusiasm alone will not get the project completed! A team leader needs to be appointed, who is ideally a member in good standing, has good managerial skills and is able to articulate clearly to keep all sections on the club updated and on board – see **Figure 18** for the qualities needed of the project team leader.

12. Planning Events

Figure 18: The Qualities Needed of a Project Team Leader

Project Manager's Role:

Team Creation	Ability to select and develop an operational team from a standing start.
Leadership	Leadership skills and management ability.
Problem-solving	Ability to anticipate problems, solve problems and make decisions.
Integration	Ability to integrate the project stakeholders (various groups within the club)
Flexibility	Operational flexibility.
Expediting	Ability to plan, expedite and get things done.
Negotiation	Ability to negotiate, persuade and make deals.
Environment	Understand the environment within which project is being managed.
Control	Ability to review monitor and apply control.
Contract	Ability to administer the project, the scope of work and scope changes.
Change control	Ability to manage within an environment of constant change.
Client	Ability to keep the stakeholders (the club environment can be quite critical!) happy.

12.2 The Project Process

The first step is to fully answer the question "is this really feasible?" It is far better for the club if that person is cautious in approach rather than foolishly optimistic.

Figure 19: Planning and Organising a Club Event – The Process

Initiation	The initiating process starts the project – this usually includes the project charter and feasibility study.
Planning	The planning process selects and develops the best courses of action to attain the objectives that the project was undertaken to achieve.
Execution	The execution process integrates, instructs and co-ordinates people and resources to implement and carry out the management plan and make-it-happen.
Control	The controlling process ensures the project objectives are met by monitoring and measuring progress regularly to identify any variances from the management plan so that corrective action can be taken as necessary.
Close	The closing process formally accepts the project and brings it to an orderly end. This involves commissioning the product and handing it over to the client for operation.

Clubs often organise events:
- To raise funds for a particular purpose (purchase gym equipment / send a team on tour / erect pitch lighting);
- To contribute to the club's current account (run a golf classic / dog race night / club Lotto);

- To enable the completion of a particular project (build a clubhouse / construct a new pitch);
- To create a supplementary account - to have, in funds, the 30% of capital required by the SCP;
- To commemorate a significant milestone in the club's development / history (an official opening / an anniversary).

When it comes to such events, some clubs seem to have "the touch" and can raise significant funding on an ongoing basis while other clubs, often after huge effort, fail to realise the benefits from such efforts and can easily be dissuaded from further efforts. Sometimes this is due to particular circumstances (a storm on the day) or the incorrect "mix" (date / venue / type of event).

Every club event is also a *learning* event, so:
- All preparations should be documented and filed for future reference;
- A Profit and Loss (P&L) account should be run from start to finish to record all financial flows;
- A full (and honest!) documented review should be held, regardless of how the event unfolded. This review should be created by the responsible sub-committee and submitted to the General Committee. Following that review, it review should be filed for future reference;

The difference between clubs with "the touch" and those that seemingly, don't "have it" is often due to a few factors:
- Good ideas in themselves are not sufficient – every idea needs someone to "own it" and to drive it;
- Clubs with the "touch" welcome change, love a challenge and are supportive of those with ideas and energy;
- Clubs with the "touch" are often fortunate in that they have people with vision, who have leadership qualities, who can persuade others regarding the feasibility of projects and who display commitment and passion

Ideally, the person who has the idea should take ownership of it, should put the initial shape on it, should be able to persuade key people as to its feasibility and then should lead the project with commitment, belief, passion and example. A half-hearted approach to a project or one that does not have "buy-in" from the General Committee is most likely to fail. Failure may then lead to recrimination and negative fallout and then become a barrier to further efforts.

12. Planning Events

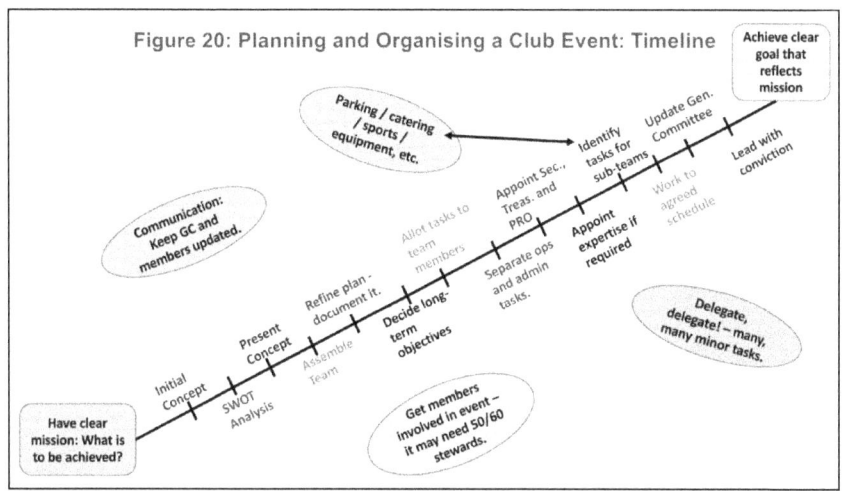

Figure 20: Planning and Organising a Club Event: Timeline

The planning and organising of a club event, which can often be significant and last over a considerable period of time, should be seen as a project. A project is a set of activities put in motion to achieve some material outcome or to introduce major change to a club achieved by:

- Defining what has to be accomplished, generally in terms of time, cost, and various technical and quality performance parameters. This can be visualised through a timeline of actions:
- Developing a plan to achieve these and then working through this plan, ensuring that progress is maintained in line with these objectives;
- Using appropriate project management techniques (breaking the project into phases) and tools to plan, monitor and maintain progress;
- Using persons, most likely club members, who have some organisational and managerial skills, under the direction of the project leader, who are given (single) responsibility for and are accountable for the successful accomplishment of the event or project;
- In club situations, the person who creates the idea and can persuade others as to its feasibility, usually becomes the team leader for the project. Otherwise, the General Committee decides that some project has to be undertaken and appoints a member, who is willing to lead it, to take on the task.

There is a lot involved in planning and implementing events. This is an area where "learning by one's mistakes" could prove costly, so it is important to have a mix of both enthusiasm and business acumen involved. To further assist here, a scenario and other materials concerning event planning are included in **Appendix 18**.

13. COMMUNICATION

The greatest problem with communication is the illusion that it has been accomplished.

(G.B. Shaw)

Anybody who has been involved in any organisation that depends on the interactions of people is aware of the importance of communication. They also know that, in the case of any problem arising, the use or misuse of communication is the most likely cause. In a world where we now have more communication platforms but less actual communication, sports clubs need to take the management of communication seriously.

Sports clubs, like many entities, often operate on the premise that "everybody knows what is going on". The problem is that this perception does not stand up to scrutiny. Furthermore, all clubs are inherently political so information and communication can be used, or misused, in pursuit of different agendas. People in particular positions can act as "gatekeepers" and can block, redirect or decide the timing of information flows, so all clubs must manage their communication processes.

Having a policy on communications is a wise move for any club. All information has the potential to enter the public domain so content and context are important. At any given time, a sports club may issue match reports, update the public on Lotto draws, place material on its website, advertise facilities, make announcements on projects and sponsors, etc. It is therefore important to have a strong Public Relations Officer (PRO) who interacts with the Secretary and the website manager so that pieces of information do not emanate from the club in an uncontrolled manner. That control can be better exercised if there is a single channel, through the PRO, for all communications. The club's website should be updated regularly with fresh news items being added to convey an image of an active organisation – websites that obviously do not receive attention are not a good advertisement for a club.

Sports clubs must exercise care when interacting with sponsors, benefactors or supporters and correspondence with such agencies should be vetted to ensure that it fits the bill. A poorly-worded letter containing typos and giving the addressee the wrong title does not impress. Good quality headed paper reflects a level of professionalism that inspires confidence. Little things matter.

New members to clubs are often left to their own devices and have to discover "what is going on" over time and through their own devices. This can be a frustrating experience but can be avoided through the creation of an *information pack* to inform the new member on matters such as facilities, rules, competitions, coaching, etc. This information pack, which could also take the form of a *club handbook* provides comfort for new members, acts as an *aide memoire* for existing members and enhances communication generally within in the club. A sample format for a club handbook can be seen at **Appendix 15.**

Communication, regardless of the medium involved, is a serious matter for clubs – the "7 Cs" should be borne in mind:

- **CLEAR:** Be sure of your purpose so that your audience will be also;
- **CONCISE:** Stick to the point and keep it brief - no "filler words";
- **CONCRETE:** Put in some solid facts – not too much detail, though;
- **CORRECT:** Titles correct? Grammatical errors? Technical terms clear?
- **COHERENT:** Have a logical flow to the message;
- **COMPLETE:** Ensure that the receiver gets all the required information;
- **COURTEOUS:** Be empathetic to the receiver. Be open and honest.

We often forget that "one cannot NOT communicate" (Watzlaweik) – every act by a club is a message to its members, its supporters and its benefactors.

A significant amount of communication is non-verbal so clubs need to be aware of how its actions might be perceived. **Figure 21** shows that communication, to be effective, must flow from top to bottom in a club – this is the responsibility of the General Committee. Communication channels should also operate laterally so sub-committees and coaches should ensure that all levels are retained in the loop of what is going on.

Another critical aspect of communication is *listening* – the General Committee should lead by example here by actively engaging with all sections of the club – failure in this regard can create "them and us" perceptions and can impede the right of all club members to have their opinions heard regularly. Feedback is important to those who oversee clubs – regular feedback is possible only where there is good communication.

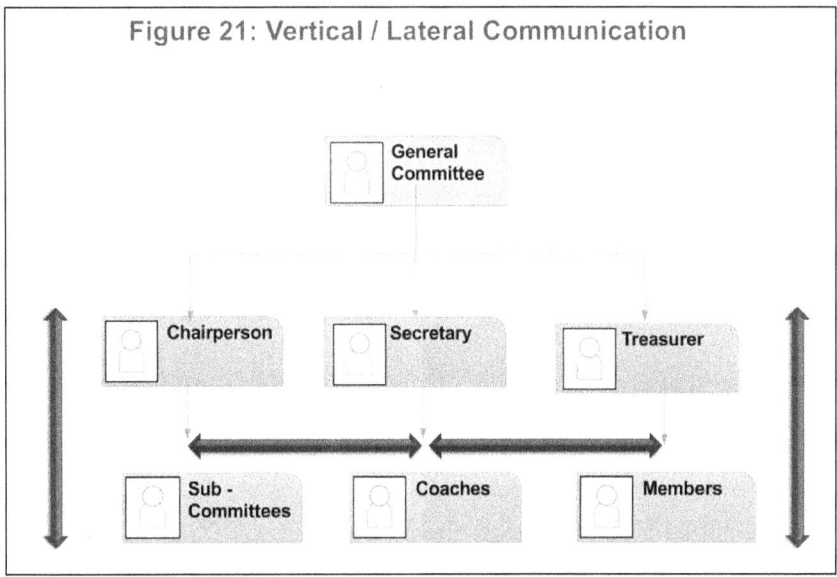

Figure 21: Vertical / Lateral Communication

Timely and accurate information and communication is critical in sports clubs. In **Figure 21**, communication – both vertical and lateral – is shown by the solid heavy arrows.

14. CHANGE

It is not the strongest of the species that survives, but the one most responsive to change.

(Charles Darwin)

Anybody who has ever served on a committee understands the mix of feelings immediately evident when *change* is mentioned. The mere mention of the word *change* in such club settings is enough for the die-hards to consider resistance before any proposed change is even explained.

However, clubs now operate in ever-changing environments, so to resist change is to be left behind. Every person on the planet has a *world view*, that view and attitude being created over time through various personal circumstances. Sports clubs with real leadership know this and so create an organisation that will satisfy the majority of opinion. This collective view is a factor in developing the club's *culture*.

Culture is often described as *the way we do things around here* (Deal & Kennedy, 1989) so it is important that the ethos of the club is positively shaped by good management. Most clubs also possess *sub-cultures*, small groups that often do not fully buy into the overall set of beliefs. Such small groups often can have their own particular agenda and can be disruptive – this is known as the *informal organisation*.

The General Committee must be acutely aware of this when any change, especially if it is significant, is mooted. They should know that change has to be managed – it is always a mistake to adopt the attitude "let's just make the change, they'll get used to it". Change that is not managed can have long-term ramifications in any voluntary organisation. So it is critical that:

- The change process is fully thought out, planned and managed through every phase;
- The communication around change must be precise, with well managed messaging.

Figure 22 indicates that the first stage of change is "awareness" This is also the tricky stage, as it depends on how people become aware: was it through the grapevine or from an official source? If this first stage is not well handled, the following process becomes more difficult. The first stage is quickly followed by the understanding of the change so the implications of the change have to be finely articulated. So it goes on – the objective is to get people to commit to the change so that they internalise it – make it their "new normal".

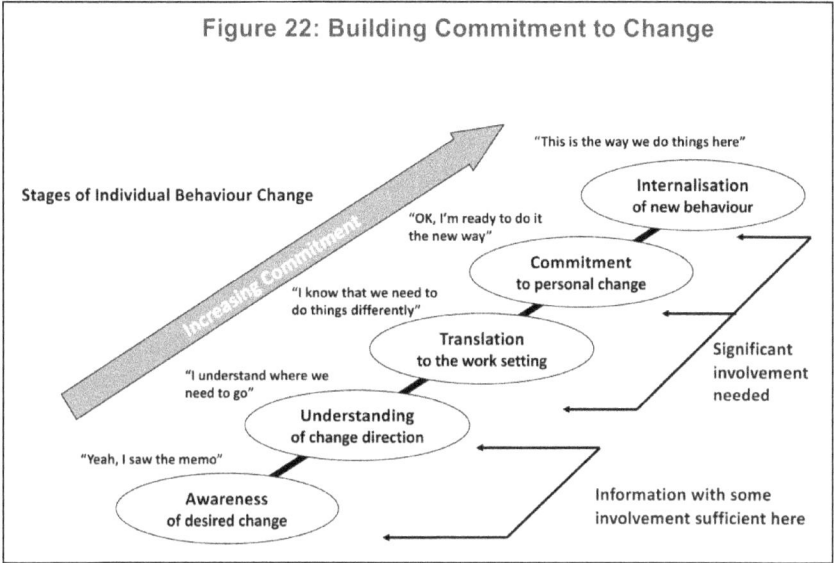

Figure 22: Building Commitment to Change

Change may come about in a club because there is a need for a new direction, a new project has to be launched, significant new rules have to be implemented or some event occurs that acts as a "trigger" for change. Whereas resistance in commercial organisations would probably not be tolerated, members of clubs can prove wilfully stubborn for some vague reason or just for the hell of it. The urge to steamroll over such attitudes must be suppressed – if the proposed change is worth it, then it is worth the trouble of keeping everybody satisfied so that there is no issue when the change is achieved.

The General Committee therefore should proceed thus:

- Establish a sense of urgency around the proposed change and highlight the opportunities to be created;
- Put together a group that has enough power (formal and informal) to lead the change;
- Create a vision to help direct the change effort and have a strategy for achieving that vision (see **Chapter 7**);
- Use every means possible to communicate the proposed change and the new direction;

- Get rid of obstacles or any structures that might undermine the proposed change;
- Plan for early visible improvement (a "quick win") in performance to prove the worth of the change;
- Invigorate the change process through small new projects and change events;
- Articulate, through good communication, the connection between the new changes and improved performance. (Adapted from John P. Kotter, *Leading Change*, 1996)

Change in a club, as in commercial enterprises, is the responsibility of the Board or General Committee. In making decisions regarding change, the General Committee must understand what performance means in terms of that club. It then must build a persuasive case to its members based on its track record in performance so that confidence is built in the process. It is said that the best way to manage change is to create it. General Committees have to innovate and to act in an entrepreneurial manner – or fall behind.

Change is not brought about by a single attempted effort – one has to persist. This has been termed as "motivate the elephant" (*Switch*, C. & D. Heath, 2010) – change is often the elephant in the room that clubs do not want to acknowledge. Change must be maintained as a "live" topic, sometimes to the point of irritating people, so change is the challenge that often uncovers leaders in clubs.

15. ORGANISATIONAL BEHAVIOUR

Setting an example is not the main means of influencing another; it is the only means.

(Albert Einstein)

Do organisations behave? The simple answer is: Yes, they do. Clubs are built on groups of people who come together because they have similar objectives in respect of the sports they follow or the good causes they wish to support. So, in most cases, the behaviour of these entities is a reflection of the members of that grouping – at the outset, at least. But then, growth and development occurs, the leaders in that grouping, being volunteers, change regularly so the ethos of the club may change. Sports clubs are living organisms so the original shape and objectives of a club may change depending on where the leadership wants to take it. It is important to remember that, in the end, the membership own the club so procedures must be established and governance observed so that the interests of that membership are protected.

That is not to say that, with the *imprimatur* of the membership, the structures and strategies of any club (remember – structure follows strategy) cannot change. Sports clubs change all the time in terms of size, type of membership, variety of activities, operating context, management, etc. Indeed, a club that does not change is in danger of becoming irrelevant. The evolution of a sports club unfolds with the consent of the members who should always make their views known through the structures such as AGMs, EGMs, committees, teams, meetings, interaction with club officers, etc.

The behaviour of a sports club can vary according to various factors:

- **Structure:** Clubs should avoid becoming too hierarchical. The General Committee should be of a size that allows it to be flexible and be capable of sound decision-making without undue procrastination. The second tier should consist of the various sub-committees required for the efficient operation of all activities. Sub-committees must be always answerable to the General Committee. The third tier should consist of the playing and non-playing members. This structure allows for short spans of control, defined reporting lines and good communication. Club roles, such as Chairperson, Secretary, Treasurer, PRO, etc. can operate freely within this structure, provided that there are job descriptions for such roles (see **Appendix 13**);

- **Strategy:** Many clubs "just do things" without having the framework to provide the necessary cohesion for collective forward thinking and planning. Any voluntary entity that does not have a strategy should reconsider that position if it wishes to serve it members into the future. A strategy is not a rigid frame but it can be shaped or changed by the members at any point to meet their evolving needs. Since the strategy is more important than the current structure, at times the structure may have to change to facilitate the implementation of strategy;

- **Operation and Administration:** The operation and administration of any club depends wholly on the integrity of its officers – the maxim "you get what you vote for" needs to be borne in mind. Members should put any internal political considerations aside when voting for club officers so that the best possible people are elected to steer the club forward. Good governance should dominate thinking when making decisions for one's club – and good administration is always the bedrock for good operations;

- **Culture:** The manner in which any club decides to behave in time will be seen as its culture. That behaviour or "the way we do things around here" is developed through the activities, the events, the stories and myths that abound in such clubs. The effect of culture can resemble a breeze blowing in trees – the effect can be seen but the breeze itself is invisible. Therein lies the danger – when a particular culture develops in a club, it can be very difficult first to see it and then, if required, to change it. So the culture that is built, or emerges, in any club has to be moulded by its leaders acting with integrity and by its members diligently observing good governance at all times. Sub-cultures can emerge in any situation and can be tolerated at times – but the club management has a duty to act if disruptive elements seek to go against the will of the majority. Caution is advised here – various members can hold very rigid views on particular matters, views that cannot be modified by persuasion. Such views, while having a nuisance value, do not necessarily constitute a sub-culture and they must be respected.

The strategy and structure of any club should be set up so that it can carry out the functions that define it. This is depicted in **Figure 23** – when the club comes up with a strategy, it then knows what it has to do. The

15. Organisational Behaviour

strategic goals are enabled through objectives and those objectives are in turn broken down into activities. But – does the club have people who are capable of conducting the activities? Is there a skills deficit? This should have been considered when "resources" were being examined at an earlier stage. If a skills gap appears, the General Committee has to find ways to bridge it, by either finding the required talent within the club or by looking outside.

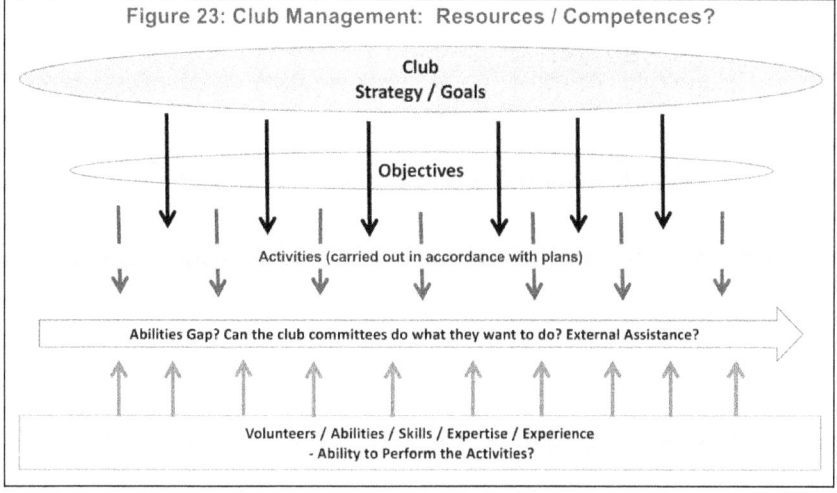

Figure 23: Club Management: Resources / Competences?

16. GROWTH

Sports clubs generally are wonderful places, islands of joyful recreational pursuits and repositories of good people who wish to address various societal issues. They are places where social norms are more relaxed and where a huge mix of people can appreciate teamwork.

Clubs give people an opportunity to enhance their social skills, to understand the value of voluntary effort and to discover abilities in communication, management and leadership. Sports clubs can act as universities in their own way because there is a significant amount of learning available if one is so inclined. There have been numerous cases of people progressing in their professions because of the confidence and management abilities picked up in their local sports club.

16.1 Growing Your Club

Members of sports clubs can be involved in an ongoing reciprocal process if they so wish – they can help their club to grow through their efforts and that improved organisation will give back in many ways – both can grow together.

Figure 24 demonstrates how growth occurs in clubs. Growth in sports clubs is a natural phenomenon, and as can be seen, a club grows through phases, from creativity to finding a sense of direction and from coordination to collaboration. These phases also can bring "crises" such as a leadership crisis, a control crisis, etc. These are normal actions in any growing club – at times, clubs do not have the leadership needed or, at other times, it may not be able to exert the correct amount of control over it activities. But the club will learn through experience, its needs will bring out the natural leadership and the development of proper processes will bring the required controls.

As with any developing personality, a sports club adapts to its environment, builds on knowledge gained and then strives to grow into an entity that can serve its membership. Progressive clubs listen to ideas and do not hesitate to fully explore opportunities – that is how organic growth occurs in clubs. But it may be advisable, before growth is considered, to evaluate the current status of the organisation to ensure that growth takes place on solid foundations. This book has provided a range of tools – those tools should now be reviewed within a framework such as the "7S Framework" (**Figure 25**).

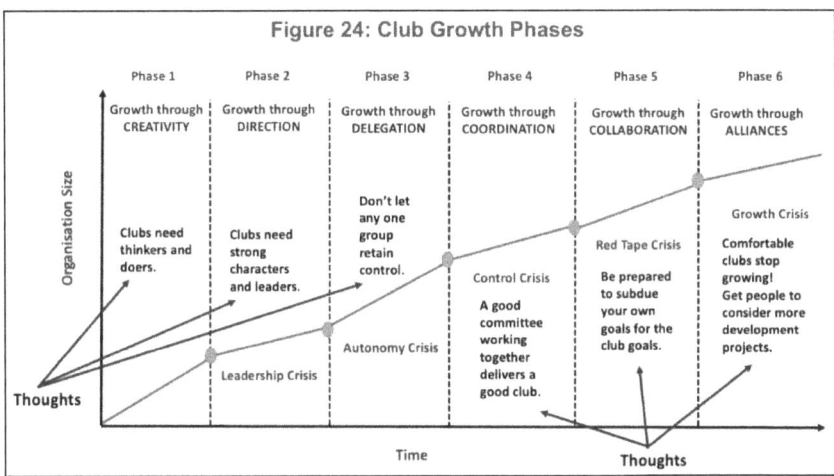

Source: Greiner, L.E. (1998), Evolution and Revolution as Organisations Grow – "Thoughts" added by Author.

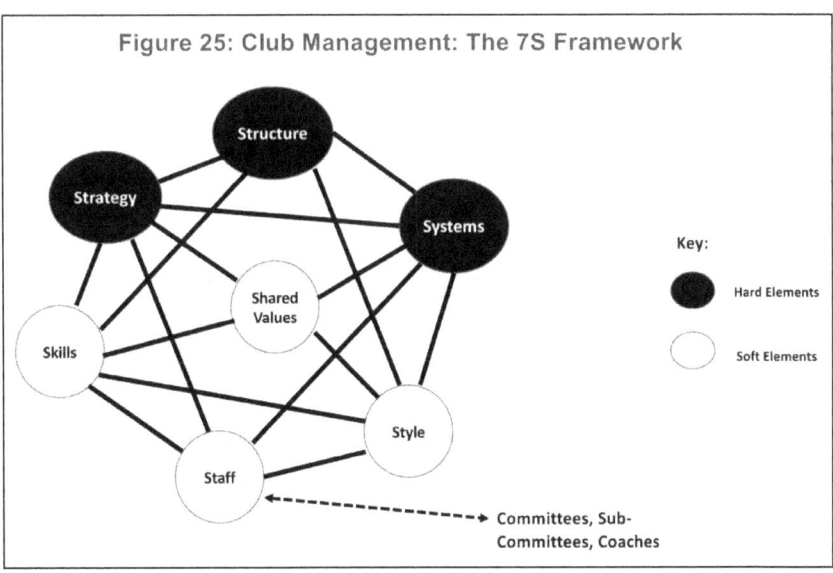

Adapted from the McKinsey 7S Framework by R.H. Waterman Jnr. & T. Peters.

The 7S framework involves:

- **Strategy:** If a club is to progress, it must have at least a shared idea and a cohesive method of making progress. Some sort of accepted plan for the club is necessary to facilitate methods for improvement – a convoluted strategic plan is not always necessary but some documented, central idea is necessary to ensure any level of efficient progress;
- **Structure:** Can the current structure support the implementation of a strategic plan? Almost every club in Ireland is run by a General Committee – with a group of Trustees in place in whom the club properties are vested – these are "unincorporated entities", although some clubs form themselves into CLGs;
- **Systems:** Are the systems currently in use in the club aligned with the strategy or would different systems improve the implementation of that strategy?
- **Skills:** Are the right skills positioned in the right places in order to implement the strategy or are personnel changes warranted? Does the club trawl the membership for more skills?
- **Staff (Members / Volunteers):** Does the club have enough members? Could particular people be encouraged to join? Are volunteers encouraged? Is there a Volunteer Policy? Is there any evaluation of club officers?
- **Style:** Is the leadership style in the club compatible with strategy formulation and implementation? Can this be reviewed?
- **Shared Values:** Does the club have a recognised ethos and values that are accepted and practiced? Is this ethos consistent with the envisaged strategy? Can these shared values be assessed / audited? Does the General Committee work to sustain a "one club" environment in which different sections do not compete?

16.2 A Roadmap for Change

Some clubs evaluate themselves through a framework as outlined in Figure 25 but for most clubs, serious, in-depth consideration of such aspects would not be normal. One hears much anecdotal evidence from clubs regarding "being in a slump" / "people entrenched in their attitudes" / "inertia" / "no enthusiasm" / "cannot see any change coming", etc. Members of such clubs can become disheartened in these circumstances and such scenarios sometimes result in members just leaving a club. However, this situation need not always be perpetuated – departing from the club is the easy option – but *it's your club* – why give up so easily? It is better to stay and vow to build a better club from within.

16. Growth

Members who find themselves, to their mind, in unsatisfactory situations in their clubs can:
- Air their grievances within various groupings;
- Broadcast their dissatisfaction and be destructive; or
- Do something to change those circumstances.

People can bring about positive change in their clubs and they can be champions of positivity as long as they realise that:
- Change and progress can take time;
- It requires ongoing action rather than perennial complaining;
- Other members have to be persuaded as to the merits of arguments; and
- Changing a ship's course in troubled waters requires a competent captain on the bridge.

The process involved here requires some courage, a willingness to put oneself in contexts wherein support and criticism can come in equal measures. The person who puts their head above the parapet is the one who usually has a strong sense that they can "get things done" and does not have an attitude of "let somebody else do it". Patience is required here – one has to fully understand exactly what "the problem" is, has to be able to articulate this issue in a positive way, have an overview of how a solution can be found and indicate a willingness to be fully involved in such a solution. Anybody who has been in this situation in a club knows that they must swallow their initial apprehensions and remain focused on the desired objectives. The solution can be found. Progress can be made. The leader will emerge to activate the "trigger". It has always been thus.

Take the first step in faith. You do not have to see the whole staircase. Just take the first step.

(Martin Luther King)

The club member who is contemplating actions to improve or progress their club should first conduct their own 7S review (see **Figure 25**) to understand how various issues can be addressed because one will find that such issues are not stand-alone areas but are connected to other problem areas.

Figure 26 reflects all the activities that, in most cases, constitute the make-up of a club. It also shows the various aspects of clubs that must be properly managed, the importance of good governance and the requirement to have good people in charge.

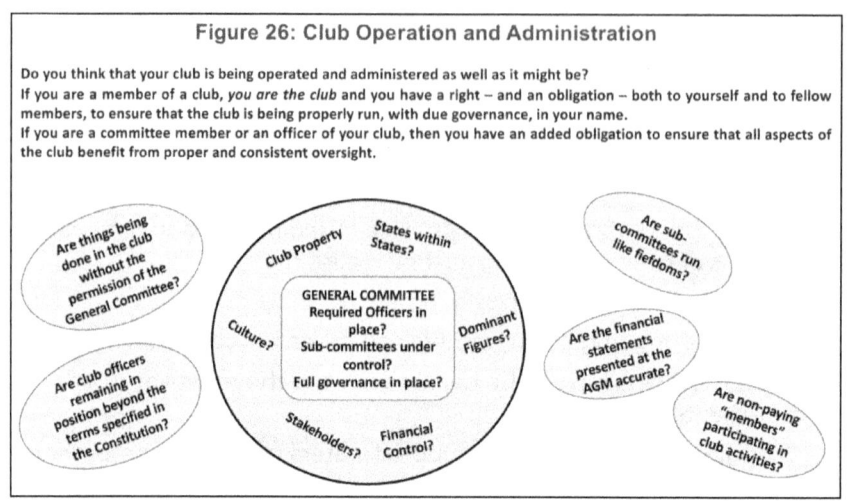

Figure 26: Club Operation and Administration

Remember that:

- Clubs are imperfect entities consisting of members from a range of personal circumstances which frame their "world view" and their attitudes;
- Clubs do not set out to intentionally harm themselves, so the evolution of the club, while currently encountering problems, eventually will meet the requirements of members;
- Those who have been elected to run the club may not always be what the club needs at any particular time. Remember – the next AGM is due in less than a year;
- Every member has a responsibility towards their club – their voice must be heard if the club is to reach its potential – committees should not construct barriers within the club;
- The club Officers have both an individual and several responsibility to operate the club in line with its Constitution and the wishes of the members;
- Good governance is not an option for any voluntary organisation – it has to operate in line with both club obligations and legal requirements;
- The Constitution of the club is its guiding force – any breach or neglect of its intentions should be immediately addressed through an EGM or AGM;
- Rules as outlined in the club's Constitution have been inserted for a purpose and must be obeyed – the stipulated terms of office for the

various appointments should be honoured, regardless of how competent the incumbents may be;
- Clubs are living organisms and can only thrive through ongoing change – change must occur on the back of inclusive discussion and agreed actions;
- The stated values of the club should be communicated regularly and be valued through action rather than aspirations.

Consider also:
- Those who think they can benefit their club should prove their worth by being elected and by working, and not just talking, for the good of the club;
- Ideas for club development can only become realities when it is agreed that such ideas merit the consistent efforts of nominated people – those who wish to convert their ideas into solid outcomes should avoid replacing one problem with another problem – every worthwhile idea should be capable of widespread acceptance;
- Any member who advocates any changes in the areas of the 7Ss should ensure that they first understand all aspects of the club's current operation and administration;
- Any member with a "big idea" should be willing to tolerate amendments or changes to the idea and to still work with other towards the agreed objectives – clubs do not need "big egos";
- Ideas for development should not be confused with "agendas" and the club should be aware of the track records of those propagating such ideas. Those who have a proven record of work in the club will have built the credibility necessary to sell a proposal;
- Proposals that are more strategic in nature should consider the resources required to run the normal operations of the club (see **Figure 27**.

Figure 27 demonstrates the intricacies involved in running a medium-to-large club. The range of activities highlights the need for skilled volunteers such as coaches, competent people who can act as administrators and a variety of members who can take on the many "unseen" tasks such as maintenance of grounds, etc. It would be desirable, in a large club, to have a properly-equipped club office, because of likely the volume of administration such as player registration, health and safety, policies, procedures, etc. The club needs people who have different skills to match different requirements.

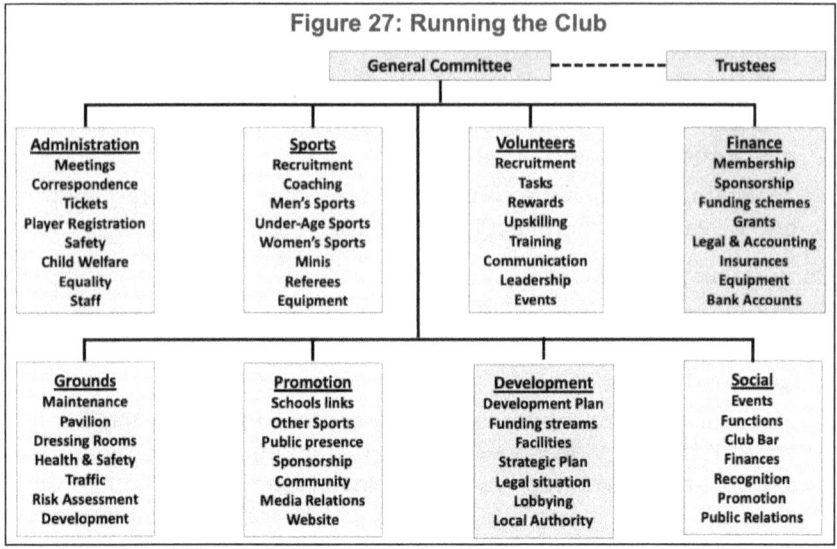

Figure 27: Running the Club

16.3 A "Club within a Club"?

There are so many areas requiring consistent attention – the sports themselves, the sports facilities and their maintenance, club development and the skills required there, the general administration and oversight of all processes to ensure that the whole system hangs together and that governance is maintained at all times. There could be an argument to have "two clubs within a club" – a paradigm wherein those who wish to pursue their sporting activities can do so in an environment where they do not have to concern themselves with any administration, fundraising, etc., while another cohort work to create that environment wherein such sporting activities can be enjoyed. This cohort could be those who have retired from sports and now graduate to club administration or, as frequently happens, those who did not possess any particular sporting abilities but who wish to be involved in the club. There is room for both types here – in fact, this should be encouraged – every club has people, often on the fringes, who are waiting to be asked to help out. Many successful clubs have been developed on the backs of people who have never excelled on the pitch but who know that they have the skills to drive their club forward. It is important for club management to continuously monitor membership so that such willing talent can be unearthed.

16.4 Governance

In every code, there are still many clubs that either do not understand governance and its full implications or which are willing to carry on in a careless manner. There are clubs operating at this moment that do not have a Constitution, do not manage membership fees, do not rotate their officers, have no child protection policies and, in doing this, show scant regard for their members. Parents / guardians of under-age club members should ensure that their children are participating in clubs that take governance, and compliance with legislation, seriously.

The best clubs have the good sense to seek out and elect those who can think and who can lead by example. Strong leadership, good governance and an environment that encourages members to cooperate on development projects, either in games or facilities, are the keys to the ideal club. Being accepted as "best in class" as a club can sometimes involve some imagination and some "thinking outside the box" – many clubs, knowing they lacked particular skills for certain positions, have gone out into the local community to target and recruit persons whose skills, expertise and experience can immediately enhance the competence of a General Committee.

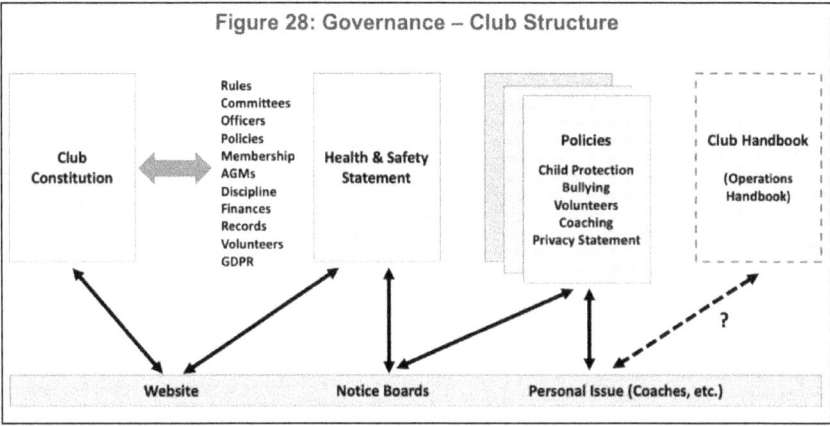

There is ample anecdotal evidence that persons were co-opted into positions such as Secretary, Treasurer or even Chairperson on their first time in the club! These clubs dared to think differently – their development is in good hands. There is nothing untoward involved here and no club members should have an issue with an intervention, if it doesn't contravene the Constitution and benefits the club. All voluntary organisations, as discussed earlier, need both leaders and managers because leaders embrace the big picture but often become irritated with detail while managers, on foot of good leadership, can take care of the minutiae.

17. CONCLUSION

This book aims to encourage those who are involved in their clubs and who want the best for them to take an overview of the overall structure, the strategy or absence of such, the leadership and the processes. Such an overview is not difficult; **Figure 29** summarises what's needed for a successful club.

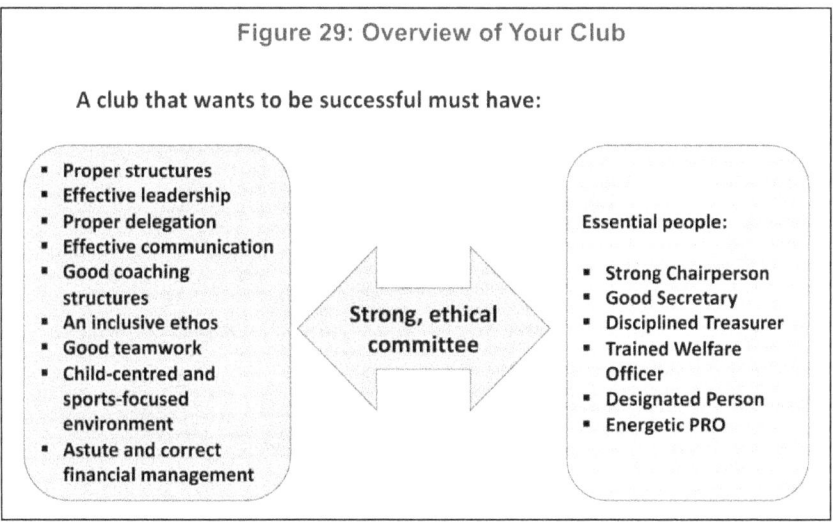

Figure 29: Overview of Your Club

All club members, regardless of code, wish their club to be seen as the standard in their particular sport. Standards are rising all the time and club facilities around the country are testament to the efforts of all those club members who are not satisfied to just stand on the side-lines but who wish to contribute to their club and their community. In more and more cases, those fine facilities are being matched by good governance so that the club members in such situations can be rightly proud of what is being achieved for both the current and future members. Being an involved member means that you have a stake in what is happening and what will happen. Remember – it's your club!

Appendix 1: National Governing Bodies & Representative Sports Organisations

Archery	www.archery.ie
Athletics	www.athleticsireland.ie
Badminton	www.badmintonireland.com
Basketball	www.basketballireland.ie
Boxing	www.iaba.ie
Cricket	www.cricketireland.ie
Cycling	www.cyclingireland.ie
Department of Sport & Tourism	www.gov.ie/en/department-of-tourism
Football Association of Ireland	www.fai.ie
Gaelic Athletic Association	www.gaa.ie
Golf	www.golfireland.ie
Gymnastics	www.gymnasticsireland.com
Hockey Ireland	www.hockey.ie
Irish Rugby Football Union	www.irishrugby.ie
Martial Arts	www.imac.ie
Olympic Federation of Ireland	www.olympics.ie
Rowing	www.rowingireland.ie
Shooting	www.irishshootingsports.ie
Sport Ireland	www.sportireland.ie
Swimming	www.swimireland.ie
Tennis	www.tennisireland.ie

Appendix 2: Club Constitution

[This template is provided as an example only. You will need to adjust it to your club's circumstances.]

ABC [Sport] Club Constitution

1. The club shall be known as ....
2. The club colours shall be .... and shall be worn in a pattern as agreed by the General Committee from time to time.
3. The club shall be the members (for the purposes of this document, "members" means both male and female members) of the time being fully paid up for a period of not less than one year and consisting of:
   3.1 Life Members, who shall be entitled to all the facilities and privileges of the club for the duration of their lifetime.
   3.2 Senior Members, who shall be entitled to all the facilities and privileges of the club.
   3.3 Junior Members, who shall be persons under 18 years of age and entitled to use the playing facilities of the club, but not to vote at an A.G.M.
   3.4 Pavilion Members, who shall be entitled to use the pavilion facilities as decided by the General Committee, but not to vote at an A.G.M.
4. The objectives of the club will be:
   4.1 To promote the game of .... in .... and its environs.
   4.2 To organise and promote games and social activities for the Club members.
   4.3 To provide such facilities as is deemed necessary to support the above activities.
   4.4 To organise such fundraising activities as the General Committee considers as fitting, including, without prejudice to the foregoing, the running of lotteries and draws.
5. The Club shall affiliate to the ....and be bound by its laws, rules and regulations.
6. The land and property of the Club shall be vested in the Trustees elected in accordance with the Constitution, and furthermore:
   6.1 The (six) Trustees shall be elected at an AGM of the club.

6.2 They shall hold office until death or resignation, unless removed by at least 75% of the members present at an EGM of the club convened for that purpose.

6.3 All Trustee vacancies created by resignation, death or removal shall be filled at the same EGM or the next AGM of the Club.

6.4 The Trustees shall, if they so wish, have access to the Club records and accounts.

6.5 The Trustees shall deal with the property / funding of the Club as decided by resolutions of the General Committee and as recorded in the minutes of meetings of that committee. Copies of all relevant documentation will be forwarded to the Trustees in such instances.

6.6 Trustees shall be empowered, by direction of the General Committee, to borrow, raise or secure funds on behalf of the Club and to execute a Deed of Charge or Mortgage on the Club's lands and premises, or to deposit the title deeds with any lending institution to secure such funds. Such funds raised by the Trustees should not exceed at any time the amount as agreed by the General Committee and recorded in the minutes of the relevant meetings.

6.7 No Trustee shall be liable for any loss not attributable to the Trustee's own dishonesty or to the wilful commission by the Trustee of any act known to be a breach of trust.

7. The management of the affairs of the club shall be under the control of a General Committee. This committee shall be elected at the Annual General Meeting of the club and shall consist of:
   - Honorary President
   - Chairperson
   - Immediate Past President
   - Club Secretary
   - Club Treasurer
   - Director of Rugby
   - Team Captains
   - Chairman, Juvenile Committee
   - Bar Chairman
   - Pavilion Chairman
   - Grounds Chairman
   - Fixtures Secretaries (2)
   - County and Branch Delegates (3)
   - Public Relations Officer

   Add or delete as appropriate as appropriate to the club structure

8. The immediate Past President is deemed to be automatically re-elected to the General Committee. Only Life Members / Senior Members of the club shall be eligible for election to the General Committee. The Officers and members of the General Committee shall hold office for a period of one year and may be re-elected. Officers such as the Club Secretary or Club Treasurer may serve for a maximum term of three years based on re-election each year. Such officers may again present themselves for election after a period of one year has elapsed since the maximum three-year service was completed. The President may be re-elected for a second year but may only remain in office for a maximum of two years at any given time. After a period

Appendix 2. Club Constitution

of at least one year has elapsed, a person who has previously served as President may again be elected to that office.

9. The General Committee shall meet at least once per month and may fill by co-option any vacancy which may arise for any reason. The quorum for any such meeting shall number seven members. Any member of the General Committee who fails to attend at least 50% of the meetings of that committee, without reasonable excuse, shall not be eligible for re-election at the next A.G.M. Any member who fails to attend four consecutive meetings of the General Committee without acceptable explanation shall be deemed to have resigned from that committee. That member will be so advised in writing by the Club Secretary. The General Committee shall then be entitled to co-opt a member of the club in his or her stead. The General Committee shall be empowered to co-opt extra members, up to a maximum of six, not elected at an AGM, to that Committee if it is felt that circumstances warrant such co-option.

10. The General Committee shall have power, by the votes of not less than 75% of its members, to make, rescind and amend Bye-laws, provided that seven days' notice shall be given by the Club Secretary to each member of the Committee. All Bye-laws, additions or amendments to same shall be noted by the Club Secretary and shall be attached to this Constitution and copies will be made available to members of the General Committee. Such Bye-laws, or amendments thereto, shall take effect upon promulgation. Under such Bye-laws, the General Committee shall appoint the following sub-committees:
    - Games Development Sub-Committee
    - Selection Sub-Committee
    - Finance and Development Sub-Committee
    - Juvenile Sports Development Sub-Committee
    - Women's' Sports Sub-Committee
    - Pavilion Sub-Committee
    - Grounds Sub-Committee
    - Social Sub-Committee
    - Any Sub-Committee required by particular circumstances

    Add or delete as appropriate to the club structure

11. The organisation of sports within the club shall be subject in all respects to the control and approval of the General Committee and may be delegated to sub-committees of persons competent in that sport.

12. The Annual General Meeting of the club shall be held not later than the 31st May in each year for the purpose of receiving and adopting Annual Reports, Statements of Accounts, electing Trustees, Officers and Committee and transacting such other business as may properly arise. Notice of such meeting will be notified in writing to all Life Members / Senior Members, either by letter, notice in a newspaper, email or social media channels at least 14 days prior to the AGM. All members shall be entitled to attend and take part at such meetings, but only Life Members / Senior Members will be entitled to submit motions, nominations and to vote. A member shall not propose a motion at an AGM unless such motion has previously been sent to the Club Secretary at least seven days prior to the AGM. Twenty per cent (20%) of Life / Senior Members shall form a quorum at any AGM.

13. Nominations for each office and for the committee shall be proposed and seconded. In the event of there being more than one nomination for any

office, the election for such office shall be conducted by secret ballot. This will also apply if the nominations for places on the committee exceed the number of places outlined in paragraph 7 above.
14. Notwithstanding the provisions of paragraph 12 above, an Extraordinary General Meeting (EGM) may be convened by either The Chairperson, The General Committee or by notice to the Club Secretary signed by at least 25 of the Life / Senior members. In such circumstances, notice will be given by the Club Secretary as in paragraph 12 above.
15. The business conducted at all meetings, be they of the General Committee, the AGM or an EGM, will be properly recorded in minutes by the Club Secretary. All such minutes will be held by the Club Secretary and passed on to every succeeding Club Secretary. Club records will not be amended unless authorised by the General Committee and such records will not be discarded or destroyed at any time.
16. A candidate for membership of the club shall complete the proper application form (Appendix A) and have it endorsed by two Life / Senior members. The application form, accompanied by the appropriate fee, shall be submitted to the General Committee. Submission of the fee does not guarantee membership. The General Committee will consider such application and inform the applicant, through the Club Secretary, of their decision. If the applicant is accepted as a member, that person will be supplied with the current club information pack by the Club Secretary. The club will operate a policy of non-discrimination of any kind when considering candidates for membership.
17. The membership subscription for the aforementioned members will be determined by the body of members attending the Annual General Meeting. That membership fee shall be payable to the club by all members prior to the 30th September of each year.
18. Any member whose annual subscription has not been paid by the appointed date of 30th September of each year is deemed to no longer be a member of the club and shall not be eligible to participate in club activities or to partake of any of the privileges attached to members.
19. The General Committee shall be entitled to determine the membership of any member in the following circumstances:
    - If a member's subscription has not been paid by the appointed date of 30th September
    - If a member is deemed to be in breach of the provisions of these rules
    - If a member's conduct is deemed to bring the club into disrepute
20. Any member who is either suspended or expelled under the terms of paragraph 19 above will have the right to appeal to the General Committee. In the event of such appeal, the Chairman will appoint three members of the General Committee to hear any such appeal within seven (7) days and to make recommendations to the General Committee. The General Committee will then make a final and binding decision on the matter within fourteen (14) days.
21. The club will maintain a website at www.abcsportsclub.com. The General Committee will appoint a person or persons to update and maintain the club website and only those persons will have "administrator" status on the website. The content of the website will at all times reflect the standards and ethos of the club.

Appendix 2. Club Constitution

22. The club name, crest, logo, colours and website will remain the intellectual property of ABC [Sport] Club and may not be used by any serving or past members for any purpose other than the agreed purposes of the club.
23. The Chairperson, who shall be elected at an AGM, will chair all meetings of the General Committee. He / She will appoint the President as deputy chairman if they are to be absent from any meeting. The Chairman will set the calendar of meetings and determine the agenda for such meetings, ensuring that the business of the club is pursued in a proper manner. The detailed duties of the Chairperson may be outlined in a Job Description as agreed by the General Committee.
24. The Club Secretary will take note of all the business conducted at meetings of the General Committee. He / She will present minutes based on those notes at each ensuing meeting and have such minutes signed off. The Secretary will be responsible for the safe custody of those minutes and any other records entrusted to their care. They will maintain all correspondence and respond to correspondence as directed. The detailed duties of the Club Secretary may be outlined in a Job Description as agreed by the General Committee.
25. The Club Treasurer will ensure that all cash receipts and disbursements are properly recorded and that proper accounts of all financial matters are maintained. He / She will ensure that any sub-committee which collects or spends money will maintain proper accounts and present those accounts to them on a monthly basis. The Club Treasurer will be a co-signatory on any bank account being operated by a sub-committee. The Club Treasurer will deal with the club's bank and ensure that financial movements are reconciled. He / She will also ensure that properly audited annual accounts are prepared for examination and adoption at the AGM of the club. The detailed duties of the Club Treasurer may be outlined in a Job Description as agreed by the General Committee.
26. The captain of the senior team, who shall also be the Club Captain, shall be elected at the AGM. That AGM may also make provision for the Club Captain to be elected by the body of players in the wake of that AGM. All other captains shall be similarly elected.
27. The club will promote best practice in children's sport. The club shall comply with the provisions of the *Children First Act, 2015* and with the provisions of the *National Sports Policy 2018 – 2027*.
28. Expenses incurred by any officer or member of the club while performing duties on behalf of the club may be claimed from the Club Treasurer, provided that such payment had been agreed by the General Committee beforehand.
29. Both alcoholic and non-alcoholic drinks may be supplied, through the club bar, to members and to non-members of the club who may be invited onto the premises on the occasion of various functions. The General Committee will ensure that the operation of the bar is in accordance with the licencing laws currently in force, and that related legislation (for example, smoking ban) is also complied with. (delete if not applicable)
30. No persons shall become honorary members of the club or be relieved of the payment of the annual subscription except in the case of Honorary Life Vice-Presidents. The General Committee shall nominate such persons as they see fit for such positions at an AGM and that body shall unanimously confer such honour on the person or persons nominated.

31. Members wishing to propose alterations or additions to these rules must give notice of such proposal to the Club Secretary not later than 14 days prior to an AGM, or may do so by having an EGM called for that purpose.
32. The General Committee shall have the power of deciding all questions not provided for in these rules, subject to appeal to an AGM or EGM

ABC [Sport] Club
Bye Laws

1. President

The President shall be elected at the AGM and shall:

- Primarily hold an honorary position in the club.
- Be the club's representative at all internal and external functions.
- Be a member of the General Committee and contribute to policy creation.
- Act as chairperson of the General Committee in the absence of the Chairperson.
- Provide advice and assistance to any of the Officers of the General Committee as required.
- Provide liaison and communication between the various sections of the club.
- Act as a member of any sub-committee, if requested, and if such request is deemed suitable by the President.
- Contribute to the general standards of the club and provide an understanding of the ethos and codes of conduct required.

2. Chairperson

The Chairperson shall be elected at the AGM and shall:

- Hold primary executive responsibility for the everyday running of the club.
- Call all meetings of the General Committee, AGMs, EGMs, particular sub-committee meetings, etc., see that those meetings carry out their business in a proper manner and that minutes are properly recorded.
- Chair the regular meetings of the General Committee and ensure that its business is properly conducted.
- Act as chairperson or member of any particular sub-committee set up for any particular purpose.
- Liaise with the other Officers of the General Committee and ensure that the duties of those Officers are being carried out.
- Represent the club at internal and external functions in the absence of the President.
- Provide advice / direction to any sub-committees as required.
- Contribute to all policy-making decisions and to all decisions which may have significant financial implications.
- Monitor the activities in the various sections of the club and ensure that the club's espoused standards are being maintained.
- Maintain close liaison with the Club Treasurer to ensure that all financial matters are being properly conducted.

Appendix 2. Club Constitution

- Act as a mediator in the event that disagreement arises between particular sub-committees or sections.
- Carry out the overall duties of the position of Chairperson in a manner that is befitting and in keeping with the ethos of the club.

3. Club Secretary

The Club Secretary shall be elected at the AGM and shall:

- Act as secretary to all meetings of the General Committee, AGMs, EGMs, and any particular sub-committee meeting, if requested by the Chairperson.
- Record the minutes of all meetings which require the attendance of the Secretary, ensure that such minutes are securely held and that they are handed over in good order to the incoming Secretary.
- Ensure that all correspondence received by the club is brought to the attention of the General Committee and that it is subsequently held in similar manner to the club's minutes.
- Ensure that all reactions / replies to incoming correspondence, as directed by the General Committee, are promptly attended to and that club notepaper is used in all such instances.
- Ensure that correspondence initiated by the General Committee is promptly attended to and that it reflects the views / decisions of that committee.
- Ensure that all members are properly notified by post of any AGM, EGM or any particular meeting where the General Committee feel that a body of members is required.
- Control the acquisition of match tickets and ensure that all match tickets are distributed strictly in accordance with any rules laid down by the General Committee from time to time, if this task is not given to a particular member.
- Act as an Officer of the club and provide advice / assistance to the Chairperson as required. Contribute to decisions and policy-making.
- Following the AGM, notify all categories of members, except Life Members, of the membership fee structure for the coming year and indicate the date by which such fees should be paid. Keep a record of membership fees received and update the General Committee in this regard.
- Issue notices to members / sections of the club as required by the General Committee.

4. Club Treasurer

The Club Treasurer shall be elected at the AGM and shall:

- Ensure that all financial matters relating to the club are properly controlled and recorded and that proper accounting measures are kept in place.
- Ensure that any sub-committee or section of the club that collects money in any fashion provides an account of same at the end of the relevant month.
- Provide a verbal report on the club's financial situation at each meeting of the General Committee and provide a written financial statement to that committee at the end of each calendar month.
- Contribute as an Officer of the General Committee to decisions and policy-making.

- Ensure that all sub-committees provide a monthly statement of their financial activities. Report to the General Committee where this does not happen.
- Ensure that all of the financial matters of the club are treated in a confidential manner.
- Report immediately to the Chairperson, if there is any doubt about any financial matter.
- Receive all membership fees from the Club Secretary and lodge same in the appropriate account. Report to the General Committee on outstanding membership fees.
- Lodge all monies received from the various activities of the club to the appropriate accounts in the club's bank. Liaise with the club's bank, get regular statements and check that those statements reflect the club's financial activities.
- Allow certain members of the General Committee to collect, record and lodge particular monies (for example, Bar, All-Weather Pitches) on behalf of the club, but monitor the bank statements to see that these are properly reconciled.
- Not allow any Officer, Sub-Committee or Member of the club to spend money or to commit to expenditure on behalf of the club. All spending, financial arrangements and commitments must be cleared by the General Committee.
- Ensure that club cheque books are securely kept and that cheques are signed by the authorised signatories only.
- Liaise with the club's auditors and provide documentation on an ongoing basis so that proper annual accounts can be provided. In such instances, copies must be made of such documentation and retained by the Treasurer.
- Ensure that properly audited accounts are presented to the A.G.M. and that explanations of aspects of the accounts are available to members.

5. Director of [Sport]

The Director of [Sport] shall be elected at the AGM and shall:

- Carry out the club's policy on the development of [sport] as decided by the General Committee.
- Act as an Officer of the General Committee and contribute to general decision-making through that body.
- Give direction to the various sections, such as senior teams, women's, under-age, etc., so that policy is properly disseminated to all levels.
- Chair the [Sport] Sub-Committee so that policy is understood and translated into practical action.
- Act as a member of the Selection Sub-Committee.
- Take responsibility for the recruitment of players to the club.
- Provide proper forward planning so that coaches for the various levels are pre-selected and receive adequate training in coaching skills.
- Report to the General Committee on ongoing [sport] activities and provide advice on any problem areas.
- Liaise with the Club Coach and team captains on matters such as playing facilities, equipment, playing gear, etc.

Appendix 2. Club Constitution

- Ensure that all competitive games at 1st XV, 2nd XV, Women's and U-20 level are observed so that playing standards are properly monitored and adjusted.
- Ensure, through the Juvenile Chairman, that [sport] in local schools is being properly supported.
- Liaise with the Fixture Secretaries and Captains so that best use is made of the facilities of the club during the season.
- Make recommendations to the General Committee on any area where it is felt that the game of [sport] can be improved.
- Liaise with the Development Officers so that the club is kept aware of ongoing trends within the province.

6. Games Development Sub-Committee

This sub-committee shall comprise of the Director of [Sport], Club Chairperson and five other members as agreed between these two Officers and the General Committee. This sub-committee shall be responsible for:

- Assisting the Director of [Sport] in agreeing policy on the development of [sport] within the club and its environs.
- Planning the range of [sport] activities in advance so that proper structures are always in place for the advancement of [sport] in the club.
- Advising the General Committee as to how [sport] is best developed in the club.
- Ensuring that all the various sections of the club are supported and allowed to grow.
- Ensuring, through proper planning, that there are always sufficiently trained coaches available to the various sections of the club.
- Putting forward proposals for the financial supporting of [sport] activities.
- Ensuring that proper codes of conduct are maintained and that codes of discipline are understood.
- Preparing reports on the state of [sport] within the club, for AGMs or as required by the General Committee.

7. Selection Sub-Committee

This sub-committee shall comprise of the ....and two members appointed by the General Committee. They shall:

- Select the various teams in good time to prepare all players involved.
- Ensure that all games are monitored by at least one selector.
- Decide on policy for such matters as injuries and non-attendance at training.
- Ensure that all squads are properly graded at the start of each season.
- Ensure that external disciplinary hearings are attended by the players concerned and a club representative.
- Make representations to the [Sport} Sub-Committee as they see fit.

8. Juvenile [Sport] Sub-Committee

This sub-committee shall comprise of the Juvenile Chairperson and the coaches of the various under-age sections. They shall:

- Organise and be responsible for the orderly running of the under-age (except U-20) sections of the club, within any guidelines as may be laid down by the [Sport]Development Sub-Committee.
- Ensure that all dealings with under-age players are conducted within the guidelines laid down in the Irish Sports Council's *Code of Ethics and Good Practice for Children's Sport in Ireland*.
- Ensure that all under-age players are properly registered and that details of parents / guardians are maintained.
- Raise funds as they see fit, whilst complying with any directions from the Club Treasurer, to support the various [sport] activities.
- Liaise with the Fixtures Secretaries with regard to timings and facilities before arranging under-age fixtures.
- Arrange for the training, through properly organised courses, of coaches and referees
- Liaise with the Club Treasurer regarding the purchase of kit or equipment
- Take direction from the …… .in any matters relating to the promotion of [sport] within the club
- Ensure that [sport] is promoted and supported in all the local schools, both at Primary and Secondary levels

9. Finance and Development Sub-Committee

The chairperson of this sub-committee will be elected at the AGM. This chairperson will appoint three members of this sub-committee, while the General Committee will appoint two members. This sub-committee will:

- Draw up plans for the orderly development of the club and have these plans updated on an ongoing basis.
- Decide on and make recommendations to the General Committee as to developmental priorities within the club.
- Develop and organise initiatives to raise finance for the capital funding of the club's development.
- Recommend which activities should fund capital projects and current budgeting.
- Co-opt other members or appoint internal sub-committees to organise particular projects.
- Administer such areas as planning permissions, applications for grants, tendering contractors, etc.
- Monitor fundraising schemes in other organisations and provide options to the General Committee in terms of general financing.
- Provide projections and the fundraising model to support any development ideas.

10. Code of Discipline and Disciplinary Procedure

The club will try to avoid imposing rules and regulations that could in any way restrict the enjoyment and full participation of any member in the club's activities. However, the club's Constitution, Bye Laws and general ethos implies a certain standard of conduct that is expected of members regardless of their status within

Appendix 2. Club Constitution

the club. In the event of a member's behaviour being reported to a member or the body of the General Committee, the following will ensue:

- The General Committee will immediately appoint a Disciplinary Sub-Committee comprising of three members of the General Committee to investigate the matter.
- This sub-committee should report back its findings to the General Committee within 14 days. If deemed appropriate or necessary, the General Committee can request this report to be completed within seven days.
- The report should contain "Recommendations".
- The General Committee will consider the Report and Recommendations and decide if sanctions are appropriate.
- If sanctions are deemed appropriate, the General Committee will be represented by two or more Officers when handing down any agreed sanction to the Member(s) in question. A sanction requiring the expulsion of a Member will require the unanimous agreement of the General Committee.
- This procedure will not pertain to players who are disciplined by a referee in the course of a match, as this is already provided for by the (County, Province, etc.) However, if a player's conduct was deemed to be excessive in any way, the General Committee will reserve the right to instigate the disciplinary procedure, regardless of any action which might be taken by the referee or the (County, Governing Body, etc.)
- Any club member who is in receipt of a sanction from the disciplinary sub-committee, as described, may appeal the finding, in writing, to the Club Secretary within seven days. The General Committee will then set up an Appeals Sub-Committee consisting of three members of the General Committee, none of whom have sat on the Disciplinary Sub-Committee.

11. Rules governing the Sale of Match Tickets

In most instances, this club will not receive an adequate quota of tickets to satisfy the demands of members. In order to distribute such tickets in an equitable manner, the following will apply:

- The ordering, payment for, retention, sale and distribution of tickets will be controlled by the Club Secretary or a person to be designated by the General Committee.
- The Club Secretary will liaise with the (Governing Body) to ensure that the club receives its entitlement of tickets.
- Unless decided by the General Committee, match tickets will not be sold by the club to third parties. In certain circumstances, match tickets may be given by the club to a charitable organisation for fundraising purposes.
- In order to be considered for a match ticket, a person must be: a member, be involved in some club activity such as playing / serving on a committee / selling club lotto tickets / coaching / serving on the all-weather roster / doing any other voluntary work for the club.
- In order to receive a match ticket a member must: (a) order the ticket at the start of the season, (b) have his/her membership subscription paid, (c) be present at the location and time indicated by the Club Secretary or designated person to collect such ticket(s), (d) pay for the ticket before receiving it.

- A person will not be considered for the further receipt of a match ticket(s) for the season in question or the following season if it is found that: the person re-sold the ticket(s) received, or having ordered tickets, did not take or pay for those tickets.
- In any situation where more than two tickets are requested, or a particular request is made (e.g.- in the case of sponsors), the Club Secretary, or designated person, may confer with members of the General Committee for advice.
- From time to time the General Committee may decide, for fundraising or other reasons, to impose a levy on each match ticket. This will be notified to members through the club notice boards.
- In the interests of fairness and equity, a portion of the ticket allocation for any given match may be distributed on foot of a draw among those applicants who, for various reasons, are not on the primary list of ticket allocation.
- The allocation of tickets for matches is a matter for the General Committee of the club to operate. No particular section of members have any particular entitlement to such tickets.
- In certain instances the (Governing Body) or the General Committee may decide to "pair" tickets for particular international matches, to ensure that the allotment for less attractive fixtures is sold. Those wishing to avail of tickets on such occasions will have to abide by these conditions. All other conditions as described above will also apply.

12. Bar Chairperson (if applicable)

The Bar Chairperson will be elected at the AGM and will be responsible for the upkeep, maintenance and running of the club bar. The Bar Chairperson may appoint his/her own sub-committee, providing that it includes at least one member of the General Committee. The Bar Chairperson will ensure that:

- As a member of the General Committee, he/she will appraise that committee of the ongoing activities in the bar area and partake in decision-making on the bar.
- The bar area is kept secure and maintained in good order at all times.
- Functions are properly booked in, that adequate staff are present for such functions and that such functions are properly supervised by a nominated senior club member.
- The bar area is properly staffed for match occasions and that such staff are of the required age and competence.
- All monies are properly controlled and that timely lodgements are made.
- The bar, particularly on the occasions of functions, is run in accordance with current licencing laws and other legislation such as that governing smoking
- Stock is ordered in time to ensure good customer service, but in quantities that are mindful of the club's cash-flow.
- The appointed staff only, and no other persons, are allowed into the bar service area, kitchen or store.
- A roster is maintained so that members have prior notice of when they are required to supervise functions or to assist in other ways.
- The General Committee are notified of any repair or maintenance requirements.

Appendix 2. Club Constitution

- Stocktaking is regularly carried out, in conjunction with the Club Treasurer
- Every assistance is given to the Club Treasurer in preparing bar accounts for the AGM.

13. Grounds Chairperson / Sub-Committee (if applicable)

The Grounds Chairperson will be elected at the AGM and will select his / her own sub-committee, provided that it includes at least one member of the General Committee. The Grounds Chairperson / sub-committee will ensure that:

- The grounds in general are kept in good condition throughout the year.
- Pitches are used on a rotational basis so that excessive wear and tear on any one pitch is avoided.
- Pitches are mowed and lined in preparation for matches.
- Feeding, dressing and mowing of pitches is undertaken on the advice of any expertise that the General Committee may contract to provide such advice.
- The first pitch is used only for First Team matches, or other matches as may be decided by the .... and not for any other purpose such as "warm-up" or under-age rugby.
- Upkeep such as hedge-cutting or tree-cutting is carried out in consultation with the General Committee.
- Any expenditure for fertilisers, spiking, etc., is properly sanctioned by the Club Treasurer
- The all-weather pitches are brushed with the equipment provided at least once a month.
- Equipment such as mowers, lights, etc. are monitored and serviced when required.
- Activities other than .... are conducted only with the express permission of the General Committee.
- Excessive use of the pitches does not take place because of activities outside the remit of the club, such as provincial squad training sessions, matches not involving the club, etc. All such use such have the prior permission of the ....
- The changing rooms / gym are maintained in good condition and monitored so that maintenance / repairs are ongoing.
- Any unauthorised encroachment / use of the grounds is reported to the General Committee.

14. Social Sub-Committee (if applicable)

A Social sub-committee may be elected at the AGM, or if not, may be appointed by the General Committee. Such sub-committee should endeavour to include all elements of the club and should:

- Make recommendations on activities which will have the purpose of enhancing the social fabric of the club.
- Set out a Social Calendar of events, for the approval of the General Committee, no later than the 30th June each year.

It also should ensure that

- Such social activities do not impose a cost on the club, unless agreed by the General Committee, rather, these activities should be regarded as fundraising in nature.
- All proposed social functions are agreed to by the General Committee.
- There is defined responsibility for the organisation of any such function and that items such as ticket sales, hiring of bands, caterers, etc., are all properly assessed before proceeding with the function.
- There is full liaison with the Pavilion Chairperson and Bar Chairperson in respect of such functions.
- Further members are co-opted onto this sub-committee if it is felt that any particular function is beyond their resources.
- Prior permission of the General Committee is received before collaboration in any social function with any other sports club or body is considered.
- Any directives issued by the Pavilion Chairperson in respect of any function are adhered to.
- All monies / expenses associated with a function are properly represented on an Income/Expenditure sheet and given to the Club Treasurer immediately after the function.
- Functions that require particular administration, such as bar extensions, are planned in good time to carry out such administration.
- All functions being considered are in keeping with the ethos of the club and do not create offence for any member or section of the club.

15. Pavilion Chairperson (if applicable)

The Pavilion Chairperson will be elected at the AGM and may select his / her own sub-committee as long as it includes at least one member of the General Committee. The Pavilion Chairperson / sub-committee will ensure that:

- The General Committee is appraised of all activities and intended activities in the pavilion area.
- There is ongoing liaison with the Bar Chairperson in relation to functions.
- The premises is kept in good order and that there is a roster in place to tidy up after functions.
- The toilets and all other rooms are maintained to a standard that reflects well on the club.
- There is liaison with any third party wishing to use the club premises, with regard to musical equipment, decorations, etc.
- The premises is continuously monitored so that maintenance / repairs are effected in a timely fashion.
- The premises are properly secured after any tidying operations.
- Recommendations regarding improvements to the premises are conveyed to the General Committee

16. Public Relations Officer

The PRO will be elected at the AGM or may be selected thereafter by the General Committee and co-opted onto the General Committee.

Appendix 2. Club Constitution

The PRO should be a person who has an in-depth working knowledge of social media systems who fully understands the club strategy, goals and ethos and who possesses excellent interpersonal skills.

The PRO will ensure that:

- The club website is updated continuously and fully reflects the activities of the club.
- All sporting and social events concerning the club receive widespread publicity.
- Good relations are established and maintained with local press and radio and that match
- Reports and other events are adequately covered on local media channels.
- Liaison is maintained with the various sections of the club to ensure that their activities receive positive support locally.
- Correspondence with sponsors and other friends of the club is properly handled at all times so
- Beneficial relationships are maintained.
- Sponsors and other supporters receive proper recognition for their support of the club.
- All relevant parties are fully updated with ongoing and upcoming events in the club.
- The General Committee is fully appraised of upcoming events and that the implications for the club are fully appreciated.
- Invitations or letters of appreciation are conveyed to particular parties in relation to various events.

Appendix 3: Safety Statement

[*This template is provided as an example only. You will need to adjust it to your club's circumstances.*]

ABC [Sport] Club
Safety Statement

1. Policy

Our objective is to provide a safe place of work and sporting activity for all members, visitors and other agencies. This statement sets out the means by which we intend to achieve this objective. It is available to all members, visitors and HSA Inspectors. It will be reviewed annually and updated as necessary.

Signed: _____ Title: _____ Date: _____

2. General Information

Doctor:

Ambulance:

Hospital:

Fire Brigade:

Garda Station:

First Aid:

Emergency Alert Number:

3. Responsibilities

AN Other will have overall responsibility for safety matters, including:
- Identification of hazards.
- Provision of safety training and instruction.
- Creation of practical and safe operating systems.
- Consultation with committees on safety and health matters.
- Accident investigation and reporting.
- Maintenance of safety notices.
- Maintenance of First Aid facilities and maintenance / testing of the defibrillator.
- Maintaining an updated master copy of the Safety Statement and any amendments.

Appendix 3. Safety Statement

4. Consultation

The safety representative will be consulted by the General Committee and will in turn provide consultation. The consultation agenda will be as follows:
- Accident record since last meeting.
- Provision and use of protective equipment.
- Safety and health training.
- Changes to the Safety Statement.
- Any other business.

5. Risk Assessment

The safety representative will undertake regular hazard audits and will use outside expertise and advice where it is deemed necessary.

RISK ANALYSIS			
Describe the Hazard:			
Who is at risk?			
What is the risk?			
What controls are in place?			
What is the level of risk?	High	Medium	Low
Actions to be taken?			
Risk level after action?			
Responsibility for action:		Action completed on:	
Review date:		Outcome:	

6. Safety Training

The safety representative will have overall responsibility for safety training, including:
- Defining training programmes.
- Ensuring that training needs are reviewed.
- Ensuring that training is carried out.
- Maintaining records.

7. Fire Safety

The safety representative will have overall responsibility for fire safety, including:
- Emergency exits are signed and lit by emergency lighting.
- A fire alarm is installed and maintained by a specialist contractor.
- A set of instructions on what to do in case of fire is located in relevant locations.
- Fire-fighting equipment is provided and fire drills are conducted regularly.
- All coaches and committee members to be trained in evacuation procedures.

8. First Aid

The safety representative will have overall responsibility for First Aid, including:

- First aid training to be provided to selected coaches and members.
- First Aid boxes are available in all sections and are maintained by the safety representative

9. Accident Investigation and Reporting

Every accident must be investigated and a full report must be given to the General Committee.

Note: This is a minimal template – clubs should seek specialist advice in this area and should, at the very least, examine the various areas here by visiting www.hsa.ie.

Appendix 4: CoVID-19 Policy

[*This template is provided as an example only. You will need to adjust it to your club's circumstances or for other epidemics.*]

ABC [Sport] Club
CoVID-19 (or other epidemic) Policy

ABC [Sport] Club, in recognising that its members are its most valued assets and that health is fundamental to operational efficiency, will provide appropriate conditions in the club, consistent with statutory obligations and which secure the highest standards of health, and welfare within our sporting environment and provides a framework for continual improvement and healthy performance.

The main objective of ABC [Sport] Club is to protect its members and to prevent the spread of the virus.

ABC [Sport] Club is committed to conducting its affairs, without exposing members, so far as reasonably possible, to injury and ill health at the club, by adhering to the provisions of the *Safety, Health & Welfare at Work Act, 2005*, the *Safety, Health & Welfare at Work (General Applications) Regulations 2007-2016* and all other applicable legislation, codes of practice and requirements. The club recognises CoVID-19 (or other epidemic)as a serious health risk to members and is committed to following HSE guidelines throughout the duration of the pandemic.

Our CoVID-19 (or other epidemic) Policy is based on the following points:

- Continued remote activities where it is possible.
- Only those that must be in the club premises will be allowed to return there.
- Training shall be provided before any member is allowed to return to the club.
- Awareness, education and ongoing training of CoVID-19 (or other epidemic), social distancing and personal hygiene.

Summary of Key Recommendations:

- Operations that do not follow the HSE guidelines will not be undertaken by any club member
- Any member who is confirmed as a CoVID-19 (or other epidemic) case or who has developed symptoms must immediately inform the Secretary or a committee member.

- All members will be given hand hygiene solutions and adequate cleaning agents.
- All members shall be required to have the highest of hygiene standards.
- Members will be informed of their duties as per HSE guidelines for CoVID-19 (or other epidemic).
- Any member who presents at the club with suspected CoVID-19 (or other epidemic) symptoms will be asked to go home, contact their GP and remain at home for at least 14 days.
- For members who may have been in contact with another member who has been confirmed as having CoVID-19 (or other epidemic) will be contacted and asked to self-isolate at home for 14 days and to contact their GP should they develop symptoms.
- Any member who has been in contacted with a suspected or confirmed case of CoVID-19 (or other epidemic) will be asked to remain at home for at least 14 days and to contact their GP should they develop any symptoms such as cough or fever.
- Any member who has travelled outside of Ireland within the last 14 days will be asked to remain at home for 14 days and to contact their GP should they develop symptoms of CoVID19(or other epidemic. CoVID-19 (or other epidemic) measures and procedure will be followed for any member who develops symptoms of CoVID-19 whilst at the club.
- Social distancing in accordance with the current Government guidelines shall be maintained for all club activities. Where this is not possible it must be reviewed by the General Committee before proceeding.
- All members, if not already informed, will be so informed of the importance of social distancing throughout the activity periods in the club.
- A CoVID-19 (or other epidemic) officer will be appointed to ensure that all procedures are followed.
- Safety documentation must include CoVID-19 (or other epidemic) measures and controls.
- Where 2 metre social distancing is not maintained for activities over 15 minutes in duration a separate risk assessment should be conducted.
- Members should not travel to the club if they believe they have any CoVID-19 (or other epidemic) symptoms.
- Members should travel to the club alone where possible. If not, possible social distancing should be maintained while travelling, particularly while using public transport.
- This policy will be reviewed for suitability throughout the pandemic and will be updated as new HSE guidelines emerge.

Appendix 5: Child Safeguarding Policy

[*This template is provided as an example only. You will need to adjust it to your club's circumstances.*]

ABC [Sport] Club
Child Safeguarding Policy

1. Introduction

ABC [Sport] Club is committed to safeguarding the well-being of all the children and young people who may come into contact with our staff or volunteers. Our policy on child protection is in accordance with *Children First – National Guidance for the Protection and Welfare of Children* (Department of Children & Youth Affairs, 2011), the *Children First Act, 2015*, with our Constitution and our general duty of care. We are committed to promoting the rights of the child to be protected, to be listened to and to have their own views taken into consideration.

2. Purpose

It is imperative that all committee members, employees and volunteers have an ability to recognise abuse as it can be defined in many ways. Definitions of abuse are outlined hereunder.

3. Dealing with Child Protection and Welfare Concerns

All committee members, employees and volunteers of ABC [Sport] Club will be made aware of and be familiar with the childcare services and child protection policy through in-house training and they will be required to sign up to the said policy.

We will appoint a "Designated Liaison Person" (DLP) to act as a liaison with outside agencies and a resource person to any Board member, staff member or volunteer who has child protection concerns. The DLP is responsible for reporting allegations or suspicions to the Child & Family Agency, Túsla, or An Garda Síochána. ABC [Sport] Club has put in place a standard reporting procedure for dealing with disclosures, concerns or allegations of child abuse. For the purposes of our particular activities, our DLP will be our Welfare Officer (WO).

4. Reporting procedure for dealing with concerns or allegations of child abuse

4.1 Any committee member or volunteer who has received a disclosure of child abuse or who has concerns about a child should bring them to the attention of the WO immediately.

4.2 Under no circumstances should a child be left in a situation that exposes him or her to harm or of risk to harm pending Túsla intervention. In the event of an emergency where you think a child is in immediate danger and you cannot get in contact with Túsla, you should contact An Garda Síochána. This may be done through any Garda station.

4.3 Where the WO considers that a child protection or welfare concern meets the **reasonable grounds for concern criteria** outlined in Section 5 below, then the WO can refer to Túsla.

4.4 A report to Túsla can be submitted by phone, by letter or by email. All required details can be found on www.tusla.ie . If the WO is unsure as to whether the incident reaches the required level of concern, then an informal conversation may be had with Túsla beforehand to determine if the report should be upgraded to formal status.

4.5 If a formal report is being lodged, then it will be helpful to include the following information:
- The child's name, address and age.
- Names and addresses of parents / guardians.
- Names, if known, of who has allegedly harmed the child.
- A detailed account of the grounds for concern, to include details of the allegations, dates of incidents, description of injuries, etc.
- Names of other children who may have some knowledge of the incident.
- Name of the school attended by the child.
- Name and details of the WO making the report.

4.6 The WO may not submit a report anonymously as to do so would not be in keeping with the requirements of the Act.

4.7 The WO, having made a report or referral to Túsla, must inform the parents / guardians of the child concerned, unless to do so would be likely to endanger the child.

4.8 Should ABC [Sport] Club decide not to take any further action on a report or allegation in relation to this legislation, then the General Committee must inform the person who made the disclosure, even if it is the WO, in writing, as to why they acted as they did.

5. Reasonable Grounds for Concern

Examples of reasonable grounds for concern are:
- Specific indication from the child that he/she was abused.
- An account by the person who saw the child being abused.
- Evidence, such as an injury or behaviour that is consistent with abuse and unlikely to be caused in another way.
- An injury or behaviour that is consistent with abuse and with an innocent explanation but where there are corroborative indicators supporting the

Appendix 5. Child Safeguarding Policy

concern that it may be a case of abuse. An example of this would be a pattern of injuries, an implausible explanation, other indications of abuse, dysfunctional behaviour.
- Consistent indication over a period of time that a child is suffering from emotional or physical neglect.

6. Guiding Principles in Reporting

The safety and well-being of the child or young person must take priority.

Reports should be made without delay to the Child & Family Agency, Túsla, or to the Local HSE office area where child resides.

A suspicion, which is not supported by an objective indication of abuse or neglect, would not constitute a reasonable suspicion or reasonable grounds for concern.

7. How to Handle a Report of Abuse by a Child / Young Person

In the event of a child / young person disclosing an incident of abuse, it is essential that this is dealt with sensitively and professionally by the employee / volunteer involved. In such circumstances, the employee / volunteer / WO should:

- React calmly.
- Listen carefully and attentively – take the young person seriously.
- Reassure the young person that they have taken the right action in talking to you.
- Do NOT promise to keep anything secret.
- Ask questions for clarification only. Do not ask leading questions (this is not an interview), but focus on receiving a disclosure from a child.
- Check back with the child / young person that what you have heard is correct and understood.
- Do not express any opinions about the alleged abuser.
- Record the conversation in writing as soon as possible, in as much detail as possible. Sign and date the record.
- Ensure that the child / young person understands the procedures that will follow.
- Pass the information to the WO – do not attempt to deal with the problem alone.
- Treat the information confidentially.

8. Role of the Welfare Officer (Designated Liaison Person)

The WO in ABC [Sport] Club has the ultimate responsibility for ensuring that the child protection and welfare policy is promoted and implemented. The role of the WO involves the following duties:

- To be familiar with *Children First: National Guidance for the Protection and Welfare of Children* and *Our Duty to Care*, the principles of good practice for the protection of children and young people and to have responsibility for the implementation and monitoring of the child protection and welfare policy.
- To provide support to all involved parties who are dealing with / have dealt with a child protection concern or disclosure.

- To receive reports of alleged / suspected or actual child abuse and act on these in accordance with the guidelines.
- To ensure that training is provided for all new and existing staff in ABC [Sport] Club on the child protection policy.
- To build a working relationship with the Child & Family Agency, Túsla, An Garda Síochána and other agencies, as appropriate.
- To ensure that supports are put in place for the young person, employees or volunteers in cases of allegations being made.
- To keep up to date and undertake relevant training on child protection policy and practice, in order to ensure the relevance and appropriateness of the ABC [Sport] Club policy and procedures in this area.
- To review the ABC [Sport] Club policy and procedures on child protection on an annual basis and amend as appropriate.
- To ensure that systems are in place for recording and retaining all relevant documentation in relation to child protection issues

9. Protection for Persons Reporting Child Abuse Act, 1988

ABC [Sport] Club wishes to draw the attention of the staff and volunteers to the *Protection for Persons Reporting Child Abuse Act, 1998*, which provides immunity from civil liability to persons who report child abuse "reasonably and in good faith" to the HSE or An Garda Síochána.

Section 3(1) of the Act states: "A person who, apart from this section, would be so liable shall not be liable in damages in respect of the communication, whether in writing or otherwise, by him or her to an appropriate person of his or her opinion that:

- A child has been or is being assaulted, ill-treated, neglected or sexually abused, or
- A child's health, development or welfare has been or is being avoidably impaired or neglected, unless it is proved that he or she has not acted reasonably and in good faith in forming that opinion and communicating it to the appropriate person."

10. Confidentiality

In matters of child abuse, an employee or volunteer should never promise to keep secret any information that is divulged. It should be explained to the child / young person that this information cannot be kept secret but only those who need to know in order to safeguard the child will be told.

It is essential in reporting any case of alleged / suspected abuse that the principle of confidentiality applies. The information should only be shared on a "need to know" basis, which means sharing information with persons who have a need to know in order to safeguard a child or young person and is not a breach of confidentiality and the number of people that need to be informed should be kept to a minimum. If an employee has any doubt as to whether a report should be made, he / she should consult with the WO.

Appendix 5. Child Safeguarding Policy

11. Allegations Against an Employee or Volunteer

Upon receipt of an allegation against a volunteer, the WO will notify the Chairperson. If the allegation relates to the Chairperson, the WO will notify the Vice Chairperson of the allegation. If the allegation relates to the WO, then the Deputy WO will notify the Chairperson of the allegation.

If an allegation is made against an employee or volunteer, then the situation requires a two-part process – dealing with the allegation of abuse and dealing with the employee / volunteer. Where possible these two parts should be dealt with by two different people.

There are two different procedures that are followed:

- The reporting procedure in respect of the child:
    - The safety of the child is the first priority of ABC [Sport] Club and all necessary measures will be taken to ensure that the child and other children / young people are safe.
    - The WO will deal with the procedure involving the child / young person and the reporting to Túsla.
- The procedure for dealing with the worker:
    - The WO and Chairperson will work in close co-operation with each other and with the HSE and An Garda Síochána.
    - If a formal report is being made, the Chairperson will notify the employee that an allegation has been made and what the nature of the allegation is. The employee has a right to respond to this and this response should be documented and retained. Furthermore, ABC [Sport] Club will ensure that the principle of "natural justice" will apply whereby a person is considered innocent until proven otherwise.
    - The Chairperson will suspend the employee / volunteer with pay (where appropriate). In the case where the worker is not suspended, the level of supervision of the worker will be increased.
    - The Chairperson will liaise closely with the HSE / Túsla / An Garda Síochána to ensure that the actions taken by ABC [Sport] Club will not undermine or frustrate any investigations.
    - The protective measures that can be taken to ensure the safety of children and young people can include the following:
        - Suspension of duties of the person accused;
        - Re-assignment of duties where the accused will not have contact with children / young people;
        - Working under increased supervision during the period of the investigation.

12. Guidelines for General Committee / Board

The General Committee of ABC [Sport] Club will ensure that:

- Its members are fully aware of the legislation in this area and their responsibilities under that legislation.
- All employees and volunteers are made fully aware of the legislation and its requirements.
- There is always an appointed WO in place who will receive the training necessary to carry out the required duties.

The General Committee will further ensure that this legislation will be fully considered when recruiting any new staff members, that full briefings of the legislation will be included in volunteer induction and that the main points of the legislation are included in the ABC [Sport] Club Handbook.

13. Code of Behaviour

All committee members, employees and volunteers of ABC [Sport] Club must make themselves aware of the organisation's good practice guidelines and must be familiar with this policy and sign up to it:

Parents / guardians of children involved with our activities will be informed of our policy and procedures:

- ABC [Sport] Club has appointed a WO to deal with any complaints or issues arising which concern the safety or welfare of any child / young person. This person is properly trained and familiar with the procedures to be followed in the event of an allegation, concern or disclosure of child abuse.
- ABC [Sport] Club has put in place an anti-bullying policy. We will not tolerate any bullying behaviour by children / young people or adults and will deal with any incidents immediately in accordance with the anti-bullying policy when working with children and young people. Where bullying amounts to any form of abuse, it will be treated as such and be recorded and reported as appropriate.
- ABC [Sport] Club staff and volunteers will show respect and understanding for the rights, safety and welfare of children and young people.
- ABC [Sport] Club has put in place all required policies and reporting procedures.
- Employees / volunteers are cautioned to avoid working in isolation with children and favouritism.
- We will respect and promote the principles of equality and diversity and will work with all children in a culturally sensitive way within the context of the *Irish Constitution* and law and the *UN Convention on the Rights of the Child* – staff / volunteers should never physically punish or be in anyway verbally abusive to a child, nor should they ever tell jokes of a sexual nature.

14. Record Keeping

Under the *Data Protection Act*, every person has a right to establish the existence of personal data, to have access to any such data relating to him or her and to have inaccurate data rectified or erased. ABC [Sport] Club will ensure that data is collected fairly, is accurate and up-to-date, is kept for lawful purposes and is not used or disclosed in any manner incompatible with those purposes. All data in relation to child protection records collected must be stored in a safe and confidential manner in a secure, locked cabinet.

15. Recruitment and Child Protection

All advertisements, screening and recruitment for vacant posts within ABC [Sport] Club will reflect its commitment to equality. We will ensure that interviewers conduct interviews in a non-discriminatory way. Interviews will be

Appendix 5. Child Safeguarding Policy

undertaken by a minimum of two General Committee members using an agreed set of questions.

A minimum of two references (one from the most recent employer) will be taken up followed by a telephone reference check by one of the General Committee members involved in the interview process. References should be in writing and no references from family or relatives will be accepted.

ABC [Sport] Club will not employ, contract or involve as a volunteer, any person to work with children or young adults who has a criminal conviction for violent crime, sexual crime, drugs-related offences or any other offences deemed inappropriate in relation to work with children.

All workers employed, contracted to work, or volunteering to work with children through ABC [Sport] Club will be required to sign a declaration form outlining any previous criminal convictions and granting permission for vetting from An Garda Síochána to be sought. Garda Vetting will be undertaken for all ABC [Sport] Club Board members and staff.

ABC [Sport] Club will review its *Child Protection and Welfare Policy* on an annual basis. The next review will take place in [month / year]. Notification of our policy and any changes made will be displayed on the club's website at www.abcsportsclub.com.

Signed: _____ (Chairperson)   Date: _____

Appendix 6: Bullying & Harassment Policy

[*This template is provided as an example only. You will need to adjust it to your club's circumstances.*]

ABC [Sport] Club
Bullying and Harassment Policy

1. Introduction

ABC [Sport] Club will make every effort to ensure that its operating environment gives its General Committee, employees, permanent and temporary, volunteers, artists and any other parties involved in any way with club activities, the freedom to conduct such activities without having to suffer harassment or bullying from any source. All such parties should be aware that harassment or bullying is unacceptable behaviour and is in breach of the policies and ethos of this club.

Behaviour that was once tolerated by colleagues will be no longer acceptable. Behaviour that is acceptable to one person may not be acceptable to another. If such behaviour is unwelcome and unacceptable, then it is a problem. Whether the harasser intends it to be offensive or not is not the point – if the behaviour is unwelcome, it is harassment. ABC [Sport] Club will not tolerate harassment of any party involved in any way with its activities – neither will it tolerate similar behaviour by any such party.

2. The Policy

Under our policy, harassment includes harassment on grounds of gender, sexual orientation, disability, race / ethnic origin, religion, age, marital status, family status, membership of the travelling community, or general harassment or bullying.

3. Definitions

Sexual Harassment is defined as unwanted conduct based on a person's gender which is offensive to the recipient and which might threaten a person's job security or create a stressful, hostile or intimidating work environment. While it is generally regarded that sexual harassment is an offence committed by men against women, recent evidence shows that men are also victims of this form of maltreatment. Sexual harassment can take various forms:

Appendix 6. Bullying & Harassment Policy

- Verbal – jokes, innuendo, requests for sexual favours, attempts to continue relationships, etc.
- Visual – display of or sending offensive pictures, slogans.
- Physical – unwanted physical contact, from "groping" to rape.

Harassment in general may include:

- *Verbal harassment* – offensive jokes about a person's race or country of origin.
- *Visual harassment* – display of material offensive to a particular racial or ethnic group.
- *Physical harassment* – physical assault.

Bullying is repeated inappropriate behaviour direct or indirect, whether verbal, physical or otherwise, conducted by one or more persons against another or others at the club / or in the course of activities that could reasonably be regarded as undermining an individual's right to dignity. A once-off incident such as described may be an affront to dignity but is not considered to be bullying.

4. Bullying and Harassment by Outsiders

Bullying or harassment of any parties associated with ABC [Sport] Club by outsiders such as repair persons, customers, agents, clients, etc. is unacceptable and should be promptly reported by the affected party to the Welfare Officer (WO) as listed below.

While ABC [Sport] Club will have no power to discipline the offender or offenders in such an instance, the club will take the appropriate action to prevent a recurrence of such conduct.

5. Undertaking by the General Committee of ABC [Sport] Club

Any complaint involving harassment will be immediately and sympathetically investigated, initially by the WO who will, in conjunction with the Chairperson, will cause the appropriate action to be taken. Where a complaint has been substantiated, the victim will be protected and will not be required to move unless they wish to do so. Victims will be protected from intimidation, victimisation or discrimination for filing a complaint under this policy. Any persons assisting in an investigation will also be protected. All parties associated with ABC [Sport] Club will be provided with a copy of this policy.

6. Responsibilities

All those associated with ABC [Sport] Club, whether committee members, members, volunteers, players, etc. have a responsibility to:

- Ensure that their own behaviour does not cause problems.
- Assist in creating an environment where sexual harassment or bullying is unacceptable.
- Ensure that all parties are aware of and compliant with this policy.
- Report to the WO immediately if they become aware of any such instances.

7. Malicious Complaints

Malicious complaints will be treated seriously and may result in disciplinary action. In this regard it should be noted that where a complaint is not upheld, this does not necessarily indicate that the complaint was malicious.

8. Complaints Procedure

Any person associated with ABC [Sport] Club who believes that they have been harassed or bullied should:

- Consider carefully if this is indeed a case of harassment or bullying.
- Raise the problem with the alleged perpetrator and ask that the conduct should stop.
- If the point above proves difficult, seek advice from the WO.
- In any event, keep a record of any such incident in case further reference is required.

In such instance, the WO will act as follows:

- Assure the complainant that the matter will be handled with the utmost confidentiality and speed and that it will be taken seriously.
- Attempt to see if a solution can be found that may be acceptable to both parties.
- Commence the formal procedure, if a solution is not acceptable or feasible, by requiring the complainant to commit the complaint to writing.
- Provide the written complaint to the alleged perpetrator and give them two days to respond in writing.
- Advise the General Committee, if the case appears to be potentially difficult, that a formal investigation of the incident should commence, using a panel which will not include the WO. The General Committee may include external expertise on any such panel.

9. Conduct of Investigation

If the General Committee accepts the recommendation of the WO, then the formal investigation panel, with external expertise included if deemed necessary, will commence without delay. Such panel will:

- Warn the parties involved of the need for confidentiality.
- Allow the participants to have representation during any hearing if they so wish.
- Make every possible effort to expedite the matter in the shortest possible period.
- Notify both parties in writing of the outcome of the hearing.

10. Outcome

If the General Committee considers that the complaint is well founded, on foot of the panel's deliberations, then it must consider the appropriate action to be taken, whether that be disciplinary action against the perpetrator, counselling for the complainant, etc.

Appendix 6. Bullying & Harassment Policy

If either party is unhappy with the outcome of any such investigation and subsequent action, then the General Committee will be required to consider what further action may be required and may have to involve external expertise in any such consideration.

11. Policy Review

This policy will be reviewed on an annual basis prior to the AGM and such review will be considered there.

12. Welfare Officer

You should contact the WO if you wish to discuss any incidents in relation to this policy. The WO for ABC [Sport] Club is: _____

Appendix 7: General Data Protection Regulations Policy

[*This template is provided as an example only. You will need to adjust it to your club's circumstances.*]

ABC [Sport] Club
Privacy Statement

This Privacy Statement was modified on [date] and is effective from that date onwards. ABC [Sport] Club is committed to protecting the privacy of its users and strives to provide a safe, secure user experience. The information we provide in this document is designed to help you understand how we use your information and the choices you have for protecting it.

ABC [Sport] Club collects personal information about you and distributes that information to help you connect with similar sites and with similar events and to provide other services to you.

Information we collect and retain

The rights to access and use of the service are non-exclusive. We collect information that you choose to provide to us. Upon signing up to using the services of ABC [Sport] Club, you are voluntarily sharing personally identifiable information such as your name, email address, citizenship, postal address and events which you may be interested in. We also collect information about how you use our website and the areas of our website that you visit.

The resulting logs contain information necessary for analysing the use of our resources, troubleshooting problems and improving services. You do not have to give us any personal information in order to perform job searches or to read the content portions of our site. In any case, it is indicated on the website whether any personal or demographic data must be provided to use the requested service or not.

How information is used

We use the information we collect about you to deliver the services we offer and to operate and improve our service. We may use your information to contact you

Appendix 7. GDPR Policy

regarding ABC [Sport] Club updates, to conduct surveys or to provide informational and service-related communications including security updates.

We strive to provide a safe, secure environment by attempting to limit access to our database to legitimate users but we cannot guarantee that unauthorised parties will not gain access. We also cannot control how authorised users store or transfer information downloaded from the database, so you should ensure that you do not post sensitive information on our website.

Registration on the ABC [Sport] Club website leads to the creation of a profile in our database that will contain information submitted by you. Upon exercising the right to be forgotten, the profile shall be deleted. This will ensure that all corresponding personally identifiable information will no longer exist in our database or databases.

Your choices about your information

You may review and edit the personal information you submit to us at any time. Simply sign in to our website and request us to make any required changes. We will edit your personal information within 30 days of the initial request. If you change your mind about receiving email newsletters and / or marketing material from ABC [Sport] Club, you may change your preferences by logging into our website and making such a request. Each time our marketing materials are sent to you, we give you the option to unsubscribe. You may also turn off cookies in your browser. This may affect your user experience.

Other websites

ABC [Sport] Club contains links to other websites that you may choose to follow and over which we have no control. ABC [Sport] Club is not responsible for the privacy policies or practices of other websites to which you choose to link from this website. We encourage you to review the privacy policies of those other websites so you can understand how they collect, use and share your information.

We do not control the data-use practices of others who may access your information through other websites. We encourage you to review the privacy policies and opt-out choices of those third parties so you can understand how they collect, use and share your information.

Privacy policy changes

ABC [Sport] Club is committed to ensuring the most secure and private operating environment for all users of the service. We will post any amendments or revisions of our privacy policy here so that you will always know what information we gather, how we might use that information and how we protect you and your organisation's privacy.

How to contact us

You may contact us for questions or concerns about our privacy practices via email, our website form or *via* regular mail. Please visit our "Contact Us" page.

Appendix 8: Garda Vetting Policy

[*This template is provided as an example only. You will need to adjust it to your club's circumstances.*]

ABC [Sport] Club
Garda Vetting Policy

ABC [Sport] Club will maintain a policy in relation to Garda vetting as this is a legal requirement under the *National Vetting Bureau (Children & Vulnerable Persons) Acts, 2012 to 2016*.

Assessing the suitability of an applicant for any position in this club is not the responsibility of the Vetting Bureau – this is the sole responsibility of our club.

We will ensure that Garda vetting is conducted in respect of any person who is carrying out work or activity, a necessary and regular part of which consists mainly of the person having access to, or contact with, children or vulnerable persons.

Any club member who is required to complete Garda vetting must arrange this application through the Club Secretary – individuals cannot apply for Garda vetting on their own behalf; it must be done through the club.

Any person who wishes to be involved in any activities in the under-age sections of the club must have Garda vetting completed before they can do so – all such persons also must be current club members.

The General Committee, in consultation with under-age coaches and other relevant persons, will determine who should be Garda vetted according to the legislation. The *Vetting Act* defines these people as "any person who is carrying out work or activity, a necessary and regular part of which consists mainly of the person having access to, or contact with, children or vulnerable adults".

The General Committee will ensure that all club members who are interacting with under-age members understand the meaning of a "vulnerable person" under the terms of the Act, which is:

> A person, other than a child, who is suffering from a disorder of the mind, whether as a result of mental illness or dementia, has an intellectual disability, is suffering from a physical impairment, whether as a result of injury, illness or age, or has a physical disability, which is of such a nature or degree as to restrict the capacity of the person to guard himself or

Appendix 8. Garda Vetting Policy

herself against harm by another person, or that results in the person requiring assistance with the activities of daily living including dressing, eating, walking, washing and bathing.

Club members should not contact the Vetting Bureau or members of An Garda Síochána in relation to vetting and should not use the club name in this regard.

All documentation required by the vetting process will be handled by the Secretary. Payment of any fees in relation to Garda vetting will be a matter of discretion between the applicant and the club.

The club will register itself with the Vetting Bureau and complete the requirements to ensure that any applications emanating from the club will be processed without any undue delay. The club will not take any actions that might incur any breach of the *National Vetting Bureau Act, 2012*.

Appendix 9: Volunteer Policy

[*This template is provided as an example only. You will need to adjust it to your club's circumstances.*]

ABC [Sport] Club
Volunteer Policy

Our organisation understands that, in operating to achieve our objectives, the role played by our volunteers is critical. We value the contribution made by our volunteers and our policy is to support them fully in carrying out their duties. Our objective is to encourage volunteers to participate in running club activities so the club will take all necessary actions to incorporate sufficient volunteers into every aspect of the organisation. Such actions will include:

- Encouraging all coaches and committee members to seek out volunteers for various activities.
- Advertising the need for volunteers on the club website and on various notices.
- Responding immediately to every query regarding a willingness to volunteer.
- Organising induction training sessions for volunteers to ensure that they understand the club's policies on various matters.

Induction training for all volunteers will include:

- Explaining the need for Garda vetting for some volunteers and the process involved.
- Outlining the club's structures and explaining why particular actions are taken
- Emphasising the club's stance on equality, diversity and inclusiveness
- Explaining the club approach to interacting with children and the current legislation which underpins this.
- Explaining the role of volunteers and the various volunteer positions which exist in the club.
- Providing information on Health and Safety and briefing on the club's various insurances.
- Clarifying how areas such as confidentiality, photography, social media, etc., are to be addressed. The implications of GDPR also will be outlined.
- Explaining the club's complaints and grievance procedure and other aspects of the club constitution.

Appendix 9. Volunteer Policy

- Briefing on the club's ethos and values and how volunteers can support these aspects.
- Exploring the various skills that can be of use to the club and matching particular volunteers to suitable roles.
- Explaining any benefits (for example, allocation of match tickets) which may be available to volunteers.

The club will strive to create an environment that will encourage the full participation of volunteers in its activities and will support such volunteers in building a strong, inclusive organisation. We will use every opportunity to acknowledge the importance of our volunteers and we will maintain good communications with all volunteers so as to benefit from their feedback. The General Committee will take account of any concerns raised by volunteers and will also implement any positive suggestions from volunteers which might benefit the club.

Signed: _____ (Position)   Date: _____

Appendix 10: Complaints & Grievance Policy

*[**This template is provided as an example only. You will need to adjust it to your club's circumstances.**]*

ABC [Sport] Club
Complaints & Grievance Policy

Any club member who has either a complaint or a grievance will have the right, under the terms of the club Constitution, to have such complaint or grievance addressed by the General Committee. It is the policy of this club to have any such issue expedited without delay.

Any club member who wishes to have a complaint or grievance addressed should inform the Secretary, preferably in writing. If this cannot be done, the Secretary will document the details and then inform the Chairperson. Full confidentiality will be maintained during this process.

If the Chairperson considers that the matter requires investigation, then he / she will appoint three (3) members of the General Committee (the Investigation Team) to conduct this investigation. This process should be completed within seven (7) days.

The person who is making the complaint or who has a grievance must be willing to participate in the investigation – they may call on witnesses or third parties to support their account of the matter.

If another club member is involved in this complaint or grievance, then that member will be included in the investigation. That member also may call on witnesses to support their account of the matter.

The Investigation Team will document all submissions made by the relevant parties and will make a decision based on the evidence provided. That decision will then be given to all parties involved in the matter.

If any such party is not satisfied with the decision made by the Investigation Team, an appeal must be lodged by that party with the Secretary within three days of the receipt of the decision. The Secretary will immediately inform the Chairperson of the receipt of this appeal.

The Chairperson will then convene the General Committee and will request that they are fully briefed on the matter by the Investigation Team. The minutes of this meeting of the General Committee will be recorded in the usual fashion by the

Appendix 10. Complaints & Grievance Policy

Secretary. The documentation completed by the Investigation Team will be submitted to the Secretary. Full confidentiality will be maintained.

The General Committee will fully consider all aspects of the matter and the decision made by the Investigation Team. They will then make a decision on the matter, on the basis of a vote if necessary. In doing this, the General Committee must ensure that it is acting in accordance with the Constitution of the club. Alternatively, the Chairperson may appoint an Appeals Committee, with different members from those who formed the Investigation Team, to hear the appeal. The Appeals Committee will then submit their findings to the General Committee.

The decision then reached by the General Committee will be considered as final. That decision will be conveyed in writing to all relevant parties who will be informed of the finality of the decision.

The matter then will be considered as concluded by the General Committee. The complainant or the person with the grievance then has the opportunity to accept that considered decision or to take any further action as they may see fit.

Appendix 11: Equality, Diversity & Inclusion Policy

[This template is provided as an example only. You will need to adjust it to your club's circumstances.]

ABC [Sport] Club
Equality, Diversity & Inclusion (EDI) Policy

1. Our Policy

It is our policy to treat all members and all others with whom we interact, fairly and equally regardless of their gender, civil status, family status, sexual orientation, religious beliefs, age, disability, race, membership of the Travelling community or any other irrelevant factor. Furthermore, we will adhere to the legislation that provides equality in the case of maternity leave or part-time and flexible work arrangements. This policy applies to all our internal and external activities.

We believe that equality and diversity in the workplace not only benefits individual employees but enables us to better reflect the world around us, enhances our connection with our audiences, deepens our links to the community within which we work and contributes immeasurably to the success of our organisation as a whole.

2. Definitions

2.1 **Equality:** Equality is ensuring individuals or groups of individuals are not treated less favourably, on the basis of any situation that may arise within the club. Equality seeks to advance equality of opportunity without any direct or indirect discrimination, or conscious or unconscious biases.

2.2 **Equity:** Equity is concerned with promoting fairness so that everyone starts from the same place. This may include positive measures in order to achieve greater equality of outcome.

2.3 **Diversity:** Diversity means more than just acknowledging and / or tolerating difference. Diversity involves understanding, appreciating and embracing differences and practicing mutual respect for qualities and experiences that are different from the majority.

Appendix 11. EDI Policy

2.4 **Inclusion:** Inclusion is a sense of belonging; feeling respected and valued; feeling a level of support and commitment from others so that one can achieve their best at work and study.

3. EDI Mainstreaming

This ensures that Equality, Diversity and Inclusion (EDI) is embedded and mainstreamed into every aspect of the club's activities, which includes assessing the impact of our policies in these areas.

4. Recognition

ABC [Sport] Club will actively support EDI through a recognition culture in the club, where all members, employees and volunteers feel acknowledged and valued for their contributions to our organisation.

5. EDI Vision

Our vision for EDI is to be a leader and role model in equality and diversity in our sport, both locally and nationally and for EDI to be at the heart of all we do.

6. EDI Mission

ABC [Sport] Club will promote EDI and will embed these fairness principles into all aspects of our sporting activities in order to sustain the optimum operating climate.

7. Legislation

There are different legislative measures in place that protect people from discrimination. ABC [Sport] Club will apply this policy in compliance with and in the spirit of the relevant legislation.

The *Employment Equality Acts 1998–2015* outlaw discrimination in a wide range of employment and employment-related areas. These include recruitment and promotion; equal pay; working conditions; training or experience; dismissal and harassment including sexual harassment. The main type of unlawful discrimination involves the treatment of a person in a less favourable way than another person is, has been, or would be treated in a comparable situation on any of the nine grounds.

The *Equal Status Acts 2000-2015*, prohibit discrimination in the provision of goods and services, the provision of accommodation and access to education, on any of the nine grounds. The Acts outlaw discrimination in all services that are generally available to the public whether provided by the state or the private sector.

The *Disability Act 2005* places a statutory obligation on public service providers to support access to services and facilities for people with disabilities.

The *Gender Recognition Act 2015* provides a process enabling transgender people to achieve full legal recognition of their true gender and allows for the acquisition of a new birth certificate that reflects this change. The *Gender Recognition Act* will allow all individuals over the age of 18 to self-declare their own gender identity.

8. Vicarious Liability

We are aware that we can be held responsible for any actions taken by a member or an agent of ABC [Sport] Club if they should act in a discriminatory fashion while carrying out particular activities. This situation can also apply to contractors or self-employed people who may operate on the club premises from time to time. We will strive to avoid such situations by ensuring that all such parties are made aware of, or are given, our EDI policy.

9. Duties and Responsibilities:

The ultimate responsibility for having a proper EDI policy in place lies with the General Committee, which will appoint a serving General Committee member as the "Welfare Officer" (WO) for this general area. The WO will ensure that:

- ABC [Sport] Club has a relevant policy to cover every aspect (for example, Bullying and Harassment) of the current legislation.
- All such policies are regularly monitored and updated.
- All relevant parties receive training, are briefed or are given the relevant policies as required.
- There is a procedure in place to react to any incidents, reports, complaints or grievances so that remedial action is immediate and effective.
- The General Committee is regularly updated on the status of all our policies in this area.

10. Our Commitment:

ABC [Sport] Club commits:

- To create an environment in which individual differences and the contributions of all team members are recognised and valued.
- To create an environment that promotes dignity and respect for every member.
- To not tolerate any form of intimidation, bullying, or harassment, and to discipline those that breach this policy.
- To make training, development, and progression opportunities available to all members.
- To promote equality in the club, which we believe is good management practice and makes sound operational sense.
- To encourage anyone who feels they have been subject to discrimination to raise their concerns so we can apply corrective measures.
- To encourage all members to treat everyone with dignity and respect.
- To regularly review all our operating practices and procedures so that fairness is maintained at all times

The WO will inform all persons who are in any way involved with ABC [Sport] Club that an EDI Policy is in operation and that they are obliged to comply with its requirements and to promote fairness within all areas and all activities of the club. The policy will also be drawn to the attention of all stakeholders.

Appendix 12: Role of Welfare Officer / Designated Liaison Person

[*This template is provided as an example only. You will need to adjust it to your club's circumstances.*]

The Welfare Officer (WO) in ABC [Sport] Club has the ultimate responsibility for ensuring that the child protection and welfare policy is promoted and implemented. The role of the WO involves the following duties:

- To be familiar with *Children First: National Guidance for the Protection and Welfare of Children* and *Our Duty to Care*, the principles of good practice for the protection of children and young people and to have responsibility for the implementation and monitoring of the child protection and welfare policy.
- To provide support to all involved parties who are dealing with / have dealt with a child protection concern or disclosure.
- To receive reports of alleged / suspected or actual child abuse and act on these in accordance with the guidelines.
- To ensure that training is provided for all new and existing staff in ABC [Sport] Club on the child protection policy.
- To build a working relationship with the Child & Family Agency, Túsla, An Garda Síochána and other agencies, as appropriate.
- To ensure that supports are put in place for the young person, employees or volunteers in cases of allegations being made.
- To keep up to date and undertake relevant training on child protection policy and practice, in order to ensure the relevance and appropriateness of the ABC [Sport] Club policy and procedures in this area.
- To review the ABC [Sport] Club policy and procedures on child protection on an annual basis and amend as appropriate.
- To ensure that systems are in place for recording and retaining all relevant documentation in relation to child protection issues.

Appendix 13: Job Descriptions for Key Roles

[These templates are provided as an example only. You will need to adjust it to your club's circumstances.]

Chairperson

Job Title	Club Chairperson
Location	ABC [Sport] Club
Main Purpose	To act as the principal elected officer of the club, and in doing so, to provide leadership to the club, to oversee the main activities of the club, to direct the General Committee and to ensure that the ethos of the club is maintained.
Principal Account-abilities	Hold primary executive responsibility for the everyday running of the club. Call all meetings of the General Committee, AGMs, EGMs, particular sub-committee meetings, etc., see that those meetings carry out their business in a proper manner and that minutes are properly recorded. Chair the regular meetings of the General Committee and ensure that its business is properly conducted. Act as chairperson or member of any particular sub-committee set up for any particular purpose. Liaise with the other Officers of the General Committee and ensure that the duties of those Officers are being carried out. Represent the club at internal and external functions in the absence of the President. Provide advice / direction to any sub-committees as required. Contribute to all policy-making decisions and to all decisions which may have significant financial implications. Monitor the activities in the various sections of the club and ensure that the club's espoused standards are being maintained. Maintain close liaison with the Club Treasurer to ensure that all financial matters are being properly conducted. Act as a mediator in the event that disagreement arises between particular sub-committees or sections. Carry out the overall duties of the position of Chairperson in a manner that is befitting and in keeping with the ethos of the club.
Reporting to	General Committee
Created on	

Signed: _____ (President)   Date: _____

Signed: _____ (Chairperson)   Date: _____

Appendix 13. Job Descriptions for Key Roles

Secretary

Job Title	**Club Secretary**
Location	ABC [Sport] Club
Main Purpose	To carry out all secretarial duties and administrative duties as required in order to meet the full administrative requirements of ABC [Sport] Club and to fully support the General Committee in its commitments to the club.
Principal Account-abilities	Act as secretary to all meetings of the General Committee, AGMs, EGMs, and any particular sub-committee meeting, if requested by the Chairperson. Record the minutes of all meetings that require the attendance of the Secretary, ensure that such minutes are securely held and that they are handed over in good order to the incoming Secretary. Ensure that all correspondence received by the club is brought to the attention of the General Committee and that it is subsequently held in similar manner to the club's minutes. Ensure that all reactions / replies to incoming correspondence, as directed by the General Committee, are promptly attended to and that club notepaper is used in all such instances. Ensure that correspondence initiated by the General Committee is promptly attended to and that it reflects the views / decisions of that committee. Ensure that all members are properly notified by post of any AGM, EGM or any particular meeting where the General Committee feel that a body of members is required. Control the acquisition of match tickets and ensure that all match tickets are distributed strictly in accordance with any rules laid down by the General Committee from time to time, if this task is not given to a particular member. Act as an Officer of the club and provide advice / assistance to the Chairperson as required. Contribute to decisions and policy-making. Following the AGM, notify all categories of members, except Life Members, of the membership fee structure for the coming year and indicate the date by which such fees should be paid. Keep a record of membership fees received and update the General Committee in this regard. issue notices to members / sections of the club as required by the General Committee.
Reporting to	General Committee
Created on	

Signed: _____ (Secretary)   Date: _____

Signed: _____ (Chairperson)   Date: _____

Treasurer

Job Title	Club Treasurer
Location	ABC [Sport] Club
Main Purpose	To actively oversee all financial transactions at every level in the club, in terms of both income and expenditure to ensure that there is accountability and transparency in all financial activities and that the club acts with integrity on behalf of its members.
Principal Account-abilities	Ensure that all financial matters relating to the club are properly controlled and recorded and that proper accounting measures are kept in place. Ensure that any sub-committee or section of the club that collects money in any fashion provides an account of same at the end of the relevant month. Provide a verbal report on the club's financial situation at each meeting of the General Committee and provide a written financial statement to that committee at the end of each calendar month. Contribute as an Officer of the General Committee to decisions and policy-making. Ensure that all sub-committees provide a monthly statement of their financial activities. Report to the General Committee where this does not happen. Ensure that all financial matters of the club are treated in a confidential manner. Report immediately to the Chairperson, if there is any doubt about any financial matter. Receive all membership fees from the Secretary and lodge same in the appropriate account. Report to the General Committee on outstanding membership fees. Lodge all monies received from the various activities of the club to the appropriate accounts in the club's bank. Liaise with the club's bank, get regular statements and check that those statements reflect the club's financial activities. Allow certain members of the General Committee to collect, record and lodge particular monies (for example, Bar, All-Weather Pitches, etc.) on behalf of the club, but monitor the bank statements to see that these are properly reconciled. Not allow any Officer, sub-committee or member of the club to spend money or to commit to expenditure on behalf of the club. All spending, financial arrangements and commitments must be cleared by the General Committee. Ensure that club cheque books are securely kept and that cheques are signed by the authorised signatories only. Liaise with the club's auditors and provide documentation on an ongoing basis so that proper annual accounts can be provided. Make and retain copies of such documentation. Ensure that properly audited accounts are presented to the AGM and that explanations of aspects of the accounts are available to members.
Reporting to	General Committee
Created on	

Signed: _____ (Treasurer)   Date: _____

Signed: _____ (Chairperson) Date: _____

Public Relations Officer

Job Title	Club Public Relations Officer (PRO)
Location	ABC [Sport] Club
Main Purpose	To understand the club objectives and ethos and to use an intimate knowledge of all club activities to best represent the club through all available media channels and relationships.
Principal Account-abilities	Ensure the club website is updated continuously and fully reflects the activities of the club See that all sporting and social events concerning the club receive widespread publicity. Ensure that good relations are established and maintained with local press and radio and that match reports and other events are adequately covered on local media channels. Maintain liaison with the various sections of the club to ensure that their activities receive positive support locally. Ensure that correspondence with sponsors and other friends of the club is properly handled at all times so that beneficial relationships are maintained. Ensure that sponsors and other supporters receive proper recognition for their support of the club. Ensure that all relevant parties are fully updated with ongoing and upcoming events in the club. Ensure that the General Committee is fully appraised of upcoming events and that the implications for the club are fully appreciated. Ensure that invitations or letters of appreciation are conveyed to particular parties in relation to various events. Explore all marketing channels in order to increase the profile of the club and to attract further support. Ensure that communication channels are strictly controlled and that no unauthorised messages emanate from the club. Maintain connections with county, provincial and national bodies to ensure that the best interests of the club are being served at all times.
Reporting to	General Committee
Created on	

Signed: _____ (PRO)   Date: _____

Signed: _____ (Chairperson)   Date: _____

Appendix 14: Financial Statements

The financial management of sports clubs can vary significantly depending on their operational size and range of activities. A sports club can have large membership fees, income from facilities, fundraising projects, etc. and can also have a range of outgoings. Another factor depends on legal structure – if a sports club is set up as a *company limited by guarantee* (CLG), then, among other obligations, it must file annual returns with the CRO. However, most sports clubs do not operate so.

Regardless of size or structure, a sports club must carefully manage its finances – there is much anecdotal evidence of serious conflict within clubs where finances have not been properly managed. There may or may not be a requirement for an accountant but it is advisable, in any situation where there is income in excess of, say, €75,000, to acquire the services of an accountant.

For the average club, the financial model should consist of:
- Balance Sheet.
- Profit and Loss account.
- Cash Flow statement.

A small club without significant assets need not worry too much about the Balance Sheet or the Profit and Loss account (P&L), which are created after the year-end – it may be too late then! The average club should concentrate on two areas – the *Cash Flow Statement*, which should be guided by an *Operating Budget*.

An operating budget is critically important in outlining what expenses have to be met over the coming year. It is advisable to set up a three-year operating budget. The operating budget is a key defence mechanism for the Club Treasurer, who often has to fight off those who wish to spend club funds – those same people often have no idea of financials. A sports club must guard against falling into debt – it will not have the same arguments as an SME when it has to plead with its bank.

A very simple operating budget could look like the table on the next page.

Appendix 14. Financial Statements

Operating Budget

Premises Costs:	Year 1	Year 2	Year 3	Teams Costs:	Year 1	Year 2	Year 3
Rent / Mortgage:	€	€	€	Coaches:	€	€	€
Heat & Light:	€	€	€	Gym Rent:	€	€	€
Insurance:	€	€	€	Insurance:	€	€	€
Maintenance:	€	€	€	Team Kits:	€	€	€
Cleaning:	€	€	€	Transport:	€	€	€
Total:	€	€	€	Total:	€	€	€

There will be all types of other costs – the dangerous items are the "variables" such as the cost of a physio, whose fees will depend on the number of injuries suffered during a given season. Some room should be built in for such variable costs if the annual costs are to be kept within budget.

The wise club will develop a discipline that is governed by the budget – "if it's not budgeted for, we can't have it. The club budget should be built on experience rather than some vague aspirations. Once the budget is adopted, the job of working within the expected cash flow is made much easier.

The value of a good cash flow statement is knowing when a particular expense will arise and having the funds in place to meet same. This is particularly important for clubs that usually come under pressure during off-season.

A very simple cash-flow statement could look like the table on the next page.

A good cash-flow plan can serve as a good club financial planner – for example, in the above template, it is known at the start of the year when the annual insurance premium is due, so the money to meet this must be in place even if some other, less important, item has to be sacrificed.

So a well-considered *operating budget* combined with a careful *cash-flow plan* will impose financial discipline on the club. Adding a strong Club Treasurer to this mix will provide the recipe for astute financial management of the club. This is a basic requirement and should not be ignored. It is advised, if in any doubt, to get professional advice or to have a professionally-qualified financial adviser as Club Treasurer. Poor financial management can damage any club – and it can be avoided.

Cash Flow Projections Year 1

	Months						
	1	2	3	4	5	6	7 to 12
Opening Balance							
Incoming							
Membership Fees		xxxxx	xxxxx				
Association Grant				xxxxx			
Sponsor 1		xxxxx					
Sponsor 2					xxxxx		
Sponsor 3						xxxxx	
Gate Receipts	xxxxx	xxxxx	xxxxx	xxxxx	xxxxx		
Club Lotto Draw	xxxxx	xxxxx	xxxxx	xxxxx	xxxxx	xxxxx	xxxxx
Merchandise Kits	xxxxx						
Hire All-Weather Pitch	xxxxx	xxxxx	xxxxx	xxxxx	xxxxx		
Total Income	xxxxx	xxxxx	xxxxx	xxxxx	xxxxx	xxxxx	xxxxx
Outgoing							
Insurance				xxxxx			
Maintenance		xxxxx				xxxxx	
Coach Salary	xxxxx	xxxxx	xxxxx	xxxxx	xxxxx	xxxxx	xxxxx
Kit	xxxxx						
Heat & Light			xxxxx			xxxxx	
Medical Expenses				xxxxx			xxxxx
Transport					xxxxx		
Pitch Maintenance			xxxxx				
Mortgage	xxxxx	xxxxx	xxxxx	xxxxx	xxxxx	xxxxx	xxxxx
Gym Rent	xxxxx	xxxxx					
Office Costs			xxxxx				xxxxx
Total Outgoings	xxxxx	xxxxx	xxxxx	xxxxx	xxxxx	xxxxx	xxxxx

Appendix 15: Club Handbook

Club Logo

ABC [Sport] Club

Club Handbook

Issue X: Month / Year

[This template is provided as an example only. You will need to adjust it to your club's circumstances.]

Contents

1. Welcome
2. Background
3. Club Mission
4. Core Values
5. Club Structure
    5.1 Committees
    5.2 Seniors Section
    5.3 Under-Age Section
    5.4 Teams
6. Governance
    6.1 Constitution
    6.2 Code of Conduct
    6.3 Child Protection
    6.4 Welfare Officer
    6.5 Bullying and Harassment Policy
    5.6 GDPR and Privacy
7. Facilities
8. Membership
9. Affiliation
10. Insurance
11. Volunteer Policy
12. Communication
    12.1 Club Website
    12.2 Interactions with Stakeholders
13. Club Administration
14. Conduct of Events
15. Training
    15.1 Senior Training
    15.2 Under-Age Training
16. Competitive Fixtures
17. Health & Safety
18. Match Ticket Policy
19. Merchandise
20. Fundraising
21. Strategic Plan
22. Useful Information

Appendix 15. Club Handbook

1. Welcome

Our club prides itself in being an open, friendly environment in which all members, whether players or not, can both compete and socialise in a place which all can regard as theirs.

We are continually striving to improve our facilities, our playing structures, our club administration and the general social structure which is pitched at providing enjoyment and inclusivity for all our members.

The club has developed over the years due to the ongoing performance of the various teams and the commitment of those who serve the club in so many ways. We are grateful to all those benefactors, sponsors and those who fundraise towards the ongoing operation of the club structures.

We ....

Signed: _____ (President / Chairperson)   Date: _____

2. Background

This club was founded in .... for the purpose of providing the circumstances in which all sectors of the community could engage in the game of [sport] in either a recreational or competitive manner.

We are affiliated to .... and the club teams, both senior and under-age, participate in the various county and provincial competitions. We have experienced a satisfactory level of success in all competitions and at all levels.

The club ....

3. Club Mission

To promote the game of [sport] in this area through the provision of facilities and club structures so that all its members can engage in this sport at both competitive and recreational levels and, in doing so, improve the fabric of the local community.

4. Core Values

We have developed our club to high standards and we have an ethos of:

- Providing a club environment which is seen to be inclusive in every respect
- Welcoming all sections of the community regardless of ability, age or gender
- Treating all members and visitors with respect
- Conducting the club business in a responsible and transparent manner

5. Club Structure

The club structure consists of a President, a Chairperson, a General Committee, which is responsible for the operation of the club's affairs, and various sub-committees, which may be set up from time to time for the purpose of overseeing particular club activities or development projects. The full club structure is outlined at **Appendix A**.

5.1 Committees

The club is governed by a General Committee, which is elected in accordance with the Constitution of the club. Sub-committees, answerable to the General Committee, are formed from time to time in order to address areas such as finance, development, etc.

5.2 Senior Section

The senior section of the club comprises of both men and women who have either graduated from the under-age section or who join the club as senior members. The components of the senior section have their own sub-committees, their own administrators (for registration, etc.) and their own sports coaches. The contact numbers of all the relevant people here are available on notice boards.

5.3 Under-Age Section

The under-age section is spread over various age groups and therefore has more components. Some age groups may, or may not, be divided on gender grounds. Again, the various age components have their own sub-committee and their own administrators. Coaches are trained and the provisions of the *Children First Act, 2015* are strictly observed. Contact numbers for all under-age coaches are available on notice boards.

5.4 Teams

The various sports and sections in the club field teams at various age levels and in particular competitions at county, provincial and national level. Such participation may depend on the number of available players, financial capability or any particular conditions that may not be commensurate with the club's abilities.

Selection of players for the various teams is a matter for the management of such teams. All teams wear the club kit when playing in competitions. The costs associated with teams, such as kit, coaching, travel, medical, meals, etc. either are funded and managed at team level or supported by the general club finances.

6. Governance

6.1 Constitution

The club has a documented Constitution which is available to any member who wishes to see it. It is available on the club website and on notice boards. The Constitution is the reference point through which the operations and administration of the club are managed. Changes to the Club constitution can be made only at an AGM or EGM of the club.

6.2 Code of Conduct

This club does not wish to burden itself with a weight of rules or to restrict the enjoyment of the club by any member. However, the club is known for its high standards and its awareness of the need for good governance. The main rules are outlined in the club Constitution and any situation arising that may be assessed as contrary to club norms is addressed by the General Committee.

Appendix 15. Club Handbook

6.3 Child Protection

As a club, we adhere to all the current legislation in respect of child protection so that all the under-age members and their parents / guardians can be confident that they are participating in club activities in a safe and enjoyable environment. Training as required is provided to particular people such as coaches and team management so that we have the required expertise and awareness at all levels of the club.

Our responsibilities in this regard are taken very seriously by all concerned.

6.4 Welfare Officer

Our policy on child protection is in accordance with *Children First: National Guidance for the Protection and Welfare of Children* (Department of Children & Youth Affairs, 2011), the *Children First Act, 2015*, with our club Constitution and our general duty of care. We are committed to promoting the rights of the child to be protected, to be listened to and to have their own views taken into consideration.

We will appoint a "Designated Liaison Person" (DLP) to act as a liaison with outside agencies and a resource person to any General Committee member, club member or volunteer who has child protection concerns. The DLP is responsible for reporting allegations or suspicions to the Child & Family Agency, Túsla, or An Garda Síochána. The club has put in place a standard reporting procedure for dealing with disclosures, concerns or allegations of child abuse. For the purposes of our particular activities, our DLP is our Welfare Officer (WO).

6.5 Bullying and Harassment Policy

Bullying is repeated inappropriate behaviour direct or indirect, whether verbal, physical or otherwise, conducted by one or more persons against another or others at the place of work and / or in the course of employment that could reasonably be regarded as undermining an individual's right to dignity at work.

Harassment in general may include:
- *Verbal harassment* – offensive jokes about a person's race or country of origin.
- *Visual harassment* – display of material offensive to a particular racial or ethnic group.
- *Physical harassment* – physical assault.

Whether the harasser intends it to be offensive or not is not the point – if the behaviour is unwelcome it is harassment. Our club will not tolerate harassment of any party involved in any way with club activities. The club policy in this matter is available on both our website and on notice boards.

6.6 GDPR and Privacy

We collect information that you choose to provide to us. Upon using our website or connecting to any online devices in the club, you are voluntarily sharing personally identifiable information such as your name, email address, citizenship, postal address and club events that you may be interested in. As a club, we comply with all the relevant legislation governing this area. Our policy in this regard is available on our website and on notice boards.

7. Facilities

We are the beneficial owners of our premises, which contain the following facilities:
- Three full-size pitches, two of which are floodlit.
- A training pitch which is floodlit.
- Two blocks of changing rooms which contain six rooms and showers.
- An all-weather pitch suitable for six-a-side soccer or hockey practice.
- A hall which can be used for games such as badminton or for social activities.
- A large sand-pit which can be used for various training activities.

8. Membership

8.1 Senior Section

Any person can apply for membership of the club. Such application will be checked by the Secretary and, unless there are conditions that would mitigate against membership, that application will be approved. Continued membership of the club is contingent on adherence to its rules and Constitution and the payment of the required membership fee by the appointed date.

8.2 Under-Age Section

The conditions that apply to senior membership also apply to the under-age section. Further to these conditions, the permission of parents / guardians is required in particular circumstances such as the need to be photographed for registration, signing of membership forms, etc. Under-age members are required to remain on the club premises at all times in the absence of their parents / guardians. Continued membership is dependent on the payment of the annual membership fee.

9. Affiliation

If any sport in the club wishes to participate in external competitions, then that sport, in the name of the club, must be affiliated to the national body governing that sport and must abide by the rules and conditions as set by that national body.

10. Insurance

The club premises and all facilities are fully insured to the required standards. It must be understood that all members of the club must have paid their membership up to date in order to be covered by such insurance. Therefore any member, or former member, whose membership is not currently paid up cannot partake in club activities. Persons who wish to park their vehicles on the club premises should have the required insurance cover on such vehicles.

11. Volunteer Policy

Our club, as in every club, is very dependent on the contribution of volunteers so we welcome any contribution from any member of the club. Volunteers often think that they need particular skills and expertise in order to help out with club matters. This is not the case – our policy is to welcome any effort, no matter how small or infrequent, which will assist in easing the burden of operating the various systems.

Volunteers who wish to be involved in any way with children need to be amenable to Garda vetting and any other training as may be required from time to time. We would fully appreciate your help in running any aspect of the club, so yes, our policy is one of welcoming any member regardless of gender or age. Your club will mean more to you when you are part of its development

12. Communication

It is important that all club members can feel that they are fully included in the overall direction and activities of their club so we understand the value of solid ongoing communication that should permeate every aspect of what we are doing. We will use our website, social media streaming, newsletters, emails and meetings with different sections at various times so that our club identity and ethos is continuously broadcasted. We also interact with numerous constituencies during matches, fundraising efforts and social events. We also use local media outlets to report on club events and to promote our general presence in the community. The contact numbers of club officers and officials are available to any club member who wishes to air any query or concern.

12.1 Club Website

Our club operates, and will maintain, a website which can be accessed at www.abcsportsclub.com. This site is intended to give members and the general public an ongoing insight into the club's activities, structures, competitions, events and any other matters of interest to its members. We ensure that the site is continually updated and always consists of content that reflects the ethos of the club.

12.2 Interactions with Stakeholders

Our club is similar to any other club in that it has a broad chapel of stakeholders, which includes its members, players, governing sports bodies, supporters, government agencies, lending institutions, the general public, etc. The club's central tenet is to treat all such stakeholders with respect and to deal expeditiously with all matters relating to stakeholders. Our ongoing intention is to properly represent the club in such interactions and to be aware of our governance requirements under the club Constitution and current legislation.

13. Club Administration

Every successful club is underpinned by a good administrative system. The main actors in our system are the Secretary, Treasurer and Chairperson. There are different levels of administration, such as that relating to player registration, so it is not necessarily one central system. In any event, proper records are maintained and most activities are documented.

The club's paperwork is retained at the club's office or it may be kept in the homes of key members. Regardless of how the administrative system is maintained, all records continue to be the intellectual property of the club and cannot be owned by any one person. It is critical that records are not altered or amended after the fact and that documents are not disposed of without the express permission of the General Committee. This is how we administer our club.

14. Conduct of Events

Various events, apart from routine games, are held on the club premises from time to time. All such events shall have to be authorised by the General Committee, which often then delegates the running of such events to a particular person or sub-committee. The purpose of the event, whether it is for fundraising, a private party or for some specific purpose, should be made clear at the outset.

If an event is being hosted by the club but is being run by a third party, then clear, documented conditions must be agreed before any such event can take place. The club always favourably considers, on foot of a documented application, any request from a member to run an event in the club.

15. Training

Training, whether for individuals or teams, is a matter for the relevant coaches and the timings, locations and requirements for such training are publicised within the club so that other sections can plan their activities. The club may make its facilities available to county or provincial squads if such arrangements do not interfere with routine club activities. The club is also prepared to make its facilities available to other clubs, regardless of code, at times in a sense of sporting cooperation.

15.1 Senior Training

The training times and activities involved in the preparation of senior teams comes within the remit of the management and coaches of such teams. That management liaises continuously with the General Committee and any expenses or particular requirements to support senior training are agreed between team management and the General Committee before any action is taken.

15.2 Under-Age Training

The training of under-age teams comes within the remit of the under-age manager and the coaches selected for each particular age-grade. The under-age manager briefs the General Committee on ongoing activities in this area and areas such as equipment, transport to games, food, etc., are part of an overall under-age policy which is authorised by the under-age sub-committee.

16. Health & Safety

The club is very aware of its responsibilities under the *Safety, Health & Welfare at Work Act, 2005* and, in this regard, appoints a Health and Safety Officer whose task it is to ensure that there is compliance with all current legislation. A documented Safety Statement is available at various points in the club and policy documents in respect of bullying, harassment, diversity, privacy, etc. are available within the club and on the club website. All club members are reminded of their personal responsibilities under the current legislation.

Appendix 15. Club Handbook

17. Match Ticket Policy

Demand for tickets for matches at the various levels always outstrips availability so, in the interests of fairness, the General Committee agrees mechanisms whereby the allocation of tickets for such games are distributed in an equitable fashion. Various factors affect the availability of such tickets on an annual basis and such circumstances are communicated to club members in advance. The club appoints a person to oversee the distribution of match tickets according to the agreed system.

18. Fundraising

Fundraising in all its forms is an integral part of club activity because the operations involved in running a club incur quite considerable costs on an annual basis. In addition to operating costs, every club has to undertake development projects that may have to be funded over a number of years. Fundraising, if not managed in an integrated fashion, can be inefficient, may not avail of available markets and can cause friction within the club if not properly controlled. The General Committee exerts central control in this respect so that all sections of the club are treated fairly and that various activities do not impinge on each other. The club's fundraising strategy and policy is available from the Chairperson.

19. Merchandise

Our club sells merchandise such as jerseys, tracksuits, kit bags, umbrellas, flags, etc. All such merchandise is in the club's colours and is sold through the club shop in a controlled fashion. The design, ordering, marketing, sale and distribution of club merchandise is a matter for the General Committee and is not outsourced to any other party. Club members should know that official club merchandise is sold only through the club, unless arrangements are made with local shops that partner with the club. Club members may not design, manufacture or sell club merchandise unless under a formal agreement with the General Committee.

20. Competitive Fixtures

The club competes in competitive fixtures at various levels and this involves both the hosting of games and travel to games. The range of activities involved here is overseen by the General Committee but is controlled by the various management teams. Such activities involve interactions with other clubs, officials, governing bodies, travelling supporters, hotel accommodation, provision of food and facilities, etc. Costs are incurred and such expenses are included in budgets to be agreed between the General Committee and the various team management groups prior to the start of the playing season. In hosting events, the club presents a welcoming environment that reflects well on its stated ethos.

21. Strategic Plan

The club has formulated a strategic plan, which is available in the club office. This plan, authorised by the General Committee, governs the development of the club over particular periods. The strategic plan usually predicts events over periods of three years and is updated as required.

22. Useful Information

- The club premises is normally closed from 2200 hrs each night unless there is an event in progress beyond that time.
- Club merchandise may be purchased during the season on Saturday mornings between 10 a.m. and 12 noon.
- Any member wishing to hire the club facilities for a function or event should contact the Secretary at …..
- The club premises are alarmed and covered by CCTV. However, members should not leave vehicles on the club premises overnight.
- Membership application forms may be downloaded from the club website. Completed applications should be addressed to the Secretary at ………….
- Club blazers may be purchased at ……………. Club ties may be purchased through the club shop.
- The club hall or the all-weather pitches may be booked by phoning ……………..
- Businesses that wish to have advertising hoardings mounted on the club's pitches or in any other part of the club premises can have this arranged by phoning ………….

Note: This is a template for demonstration purposes only – a sports club should amend / change the contents to suit its particular requirements.

Appendix 16: Strategic Plan

Club Logo

ABC [Sport] Club Strategic Plan, 20xx to 20XX

Issue X: Month / Year

[This template is provided as an example only. You will need to adjust it to your club's circumstances.]

Contents

1. Introduction
2. Background
3. Organisational Structure
4. Vision
5. Mission
6. Core Values
7. Problem Statement
8. Methodology
9. Strategic Goals
10. Objectives
11. Planning to achieve objectives
12. Monitoring and Evaluation

Appendices:
- 1: Organisational Structure
- 2: PESTEL Analysis
- 3: SWOT Analysis
- 4: Operational Plan for Objective 1
- 5: Operational Plan for Objective 2
- 6: ....
- 7: ....

1. Introduction

Here you outline the reasons, the timings and the "trigger" for this plan. Give an overview of the importance of direction for the club, the type of outcomes to be expected from this plan, etc. Emphasise how clubs must evolve, the importance of continual change, bringing value to the local community, etc.

2. Background

Here you give a description of the founding of the club, its progress over years, some big milestones, the building of a "club brand" in the local area, etc. Don't get into too much detail but ensure that a good "story" is covered. Avoid using names if possible – it can cause friction – use titles.

3. Organisational Structure

Describe the current status of the club – is it an "unincorporated entity" or a company limited by guarantee (CLG). If it's a CLG, then outline some of the obligations, such as filing annual accounts with the Companies Registration Office and Revenue Commissioners.

Appendix 16. Strategic Plan

You can include the current committee structure – whether it's a General Committee (with Trustees) or a Board of Directors (if the club is a CLG). Your committee structure should go into Appendix 1 - *not in the main body. Again, with structures, no names, just appointments (Chairperson / Secretary / Treasurer, etc.)*

4. Vision

For example: To build on the established reputation for [sport] in this area so as to create a hinterland that will support the development of both recreational and competitive [sport] in an environment which will be inclusive and which will rank as a sport of first choice for all sections of the community regardless of age or gender.

5. Mission

For example: ABC [Sport] Club will, as a club, create the environment and the structures to positively promote the sport of [sport] at both competitive and recreational levels in this general area in order to establish [sport] as a major sport throughout the region.

The mission statement should follow the "military" format of "Who, What, When, Where, Why" – the "How" is constituted through the operations which makes the strategic plan come "alive".

6. Core Values

For example:

- ABC [Sport] Club provided a sporting environment for all ages in the local community.
- We offer a welcoming, inclusive club for all members regardless of gender, race or colour.
- Our club treats every member, and all visitors to the club, with respect and we act with integrity in all interactions with member and other third parties.

These are somewhat aspirational as against being core values – but can be worked on to create core values. Core values are an important measure of a club's intent and should be carefully created.

7. Problem Statement

The Problem Statement can be just as important (if not more so) than even the SWOT Analysis when preparing to create the strategic plan. You should be able to describe the central problem facing your club in one single statement – if you can do that, you have achieved a lot. The value of a good Problem Statement is seen when it comes to outlining the two or three (at most) strategic goals – very often, the goals can be achieved by flipping the Problem Statement coin.

A typical Problem Statement could read like this:

ABC [Sport] Club, in its current format, does not have to necessary structures, processes or membership to allow it to develop to the degree that will enable [sport] to become a major sport in the region.

Note the critical words here – structures, processes, membership – if you think about these, you will see that they are the three core areas on which the club should be developed – it would be surprising if, after you undertake analysis and come up with strategic goals, that such goals do not reflect these three areas.

8. Methodology

The methodology need not be a long paragraph – it merely describes to the reader what has been done to create the strategic plan. The suggested process would be:

- *Setting up of a Project Team with the task of creating the strategic plan.*
- *Undertaking a PESTEL Analysis (Appendix 2).*
- *Undertaking a SWOT Analysis (Appendix 3).*
- *Undertaking a Balanced Scorecard Analysis (Appendix 4).*

The methodology is important so that those who read the plan understand that the plan is the result of thought and analysis aimed at the best development route for the club.

9. Strategic Goals

A club such as ABC [Sport] Club is of a size that does not need many goals. Having too many goals is a mistake made by many organisations. Having a lot of goals usually reflects a lack of clarity (and analysis) on the part of the club.

ABC [Sport] Club probably needs two or, at most, three strategic goals. Remember that goals can be broken down into objectives so all the related aspects of one big issue can be addressed in this manner.

So, without prejudicing what goals you might create, it is imagined (going back to your Problem Statement) that your goals might look like this:

- Goal 1: To reconfigure all of the structures of the club to enable it to fully support its planned actions.
- Goal 2: To modify all processes within the club to allow it to fully facilitate all its activities for the benefit of its members and the community.

10. Objectives

The two goals above can now be broken down into as many objectives as you like – you can see that, between the two goals, the critical areas of structures, processes and membership are covered.

You now can see that, by using the two goals above, as many objectives as is deemed necessary can be broken out in order to take actions in various areas.

So, Goal 1 (Reconfigure all of the structure of the club ....) could be broken down as follows, for example:

- Objective 1: To set up administrative functions to support club operations.
- Objective 2: To set up a General Committee structure to run the club operations.
- Objective 3: To organise sub-committees to carry out particular functions in the club.

Appendix 16. Strategic Plan

- Objective 4: To elect seven (7) Trustees in whom the current and future assets will be entrusted.
- Objective 5: To consider the purchase the purchase of lands to create a permanent club structure.

It can now be easily seen how two main goals could be broken down into 10 / 12 objectives – so do not be tempted to go for too many goals – two or three goals will concentrate minds.

11. Planning to Achieve Objectives

Objectives can be achieved by forming them into concise operational plans. Such operational plans need not be complicated in any way – they can be accommodated on one sheet – and an operational plan can cover either a single or several objectives. See example:

Goal 1: To reconfigure all of the club structures to enable support of all planned actions						
Objective	Actions	Start	Responsibility	Resources	KPIs	Finish
1. To set up administrative functions to support club operations						
2. To set up a General Committee structure to run the club operations						
3. To …….						
4. To …………						
5. To …………..						

It can now be seen how the detail of the strategic plan begins to emerge. It is advisable to place such operational plans on Excel sheets – one can then use as many headings (Actions, Responsibility, Resources, etc.) as is needed – every club will have different requirements and will therefore use different headings. There is a choice here – use a separate operational plan for each objective or group a few objectives into one operational plan.

12. Monitoring and Evaluation

It is essential to monitor any ongoing plan to ensure that all actions are being carried out, that those responsible are completing their tasks, that deadlines are being met, etc. Evaluation is necessary to ensure that the agreed standards are being met, that value for money is being achieved, that the outputs are as expected, etc.

This information is necessary so that action can be taken if events are not happening in line with expectations. It will also be very useful in preparing reports for the General Committee.

Monitoring and Evaluation (M&E) can again be conducted by using an Excel sheet to gather the information. Hereunder is a very simple layout – this can be amended / changed to suit your club:

MONITORING & EVALUATION						
GOAL 1	**Start Date**	**Responsibility**	**Review**	**Progress**	**Review**	**Close date**
Objective 1						
Objective 3						
Objective 3						
Objective 4						
Objective 5						
GOAL 2	**Start Date**	**Responsibility**	**Review**	**Progress**	**Review**	**Close date**
Objective 6						
Objective 7						
Objective 8						
Objective 9						
Objective 10						

Here, at one glance, one can view all the goals, the objectives deriving from such goals. It can be seen immediately where some objective is not been achieved so action can be taken. Again, the headings here are just an example – every club will have its own needs so the headings can be changed to suit.

The journey from the high-level "vision" to the practical steps of converting objectives into actions is now almost complete – any club should be able to appreciate the usefulness of a strategic plan – it will be hard to define direction without it.

Appendix 16. Strategic Plan

One further step can now be taken – having broken the goals down into objectives, the objectives themselves can now be sub-divided into "activities" – this will give even more control to the project leader or the General Committee:

GOALS	Objectives	Activities	Start Date	Responsibility	Resources	Close Date
Goal 1: To upgrade the facilities that support each sport within the club	1: To carry out …	1				
		2				
		3				
		4				
		5				
	2: To make …. happen	1				
		2				
		3				
		4				
		5				
	3: To get planning permission for …	1				
		2				
		3				
		4				
		5				

13. Appendices

When organising documents, appendices should appear on separate pages (a page or more for each appendix). For example purpose here, a selection of appendices will be grouped together:

Appendix 1: ABC [Sport] Club: Organisational Structure

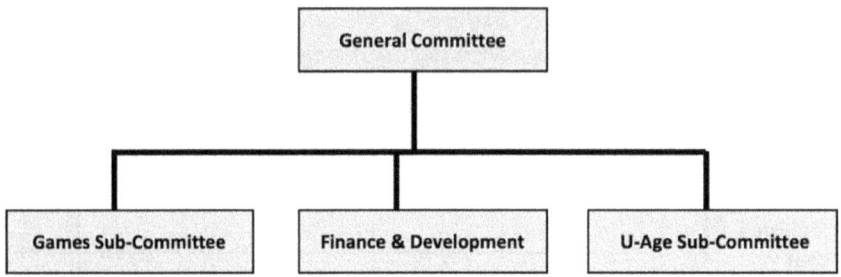

Appendix 2: PESTEL Analysis

POLITICAL	ECONOMIC	SOCIAL
For example: Current legislation Future legislation International legislation Regulatory bodies and processes Government policies Government term and change	For example: Home economy Economy trends Overseas economies General taxation Customer / end-user drivers Interest / exchange rates	For example: Lifestyle trends Demographics Consumer attitudes and opinions Media views Consumer buying patterns Fashion and role models Major events and influences
TECHNOLOGICAL	**ENVIRONMENTAL**	**LEGAL**
For example: Maturity of technology Manufacturing maturity and capacity Information and communications Consumer buying mechanisms / technology Technology legislation Innovation potential	For example: Housing situation Local legislation Residential locations	For example: Contracts Patent claims Employee legislation Health legislation Company law

Appendix 16. Strategic Plan

Appendix 3: SWOT Analysis

	Positive factors	Negative factors
Internal factors	STRENGTHS	WEAKNESSES
External factors	OPPORTUNITIES	THREATS

Appendix 17: Marketing Plan

Club Logo

ABC [Sport] Club Marketing Plan

Issue X: Month / Year

[*This template is provided as an example only. You will need to adjust it to your club's circumstances.*]

Appendix 17. Marketing Plan

Contents
1. Summary
2. Marketing Strategy
   2.1 Marketing Objectives
3. Target Market
   3.1 Customer Profiles
   3.2 Competitor Analysis
4. Market Channels
5. Implementation

1. Summary

This section should be completed last. Provide summary details of:
- Your market strategy, your objectives and how you will achieve them;
- Your target market, its size, customers and competitors;
- The channels to reach your target customers;
- The implementation plan.

Be clear and concise. This summary should take up no more than a page.

2. Marketing Strategy

Include details of:

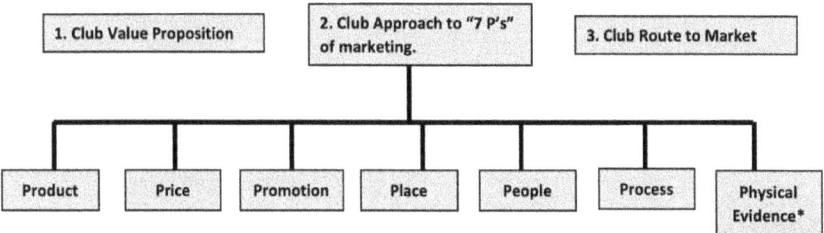

* *"Physical Evidence" provides the opportunity to outline what the club has to offer.*

2.1 Marketing Objectives

List the key marketing objectives of the club. There should be at least three objectives and ideally no more than six. The objectives should be SMART: Specific, Measurable, Attainable, Realistic and Timely.
- *(Objective 1)*
- *(Objective 2)*
- *(Objective 3)*
- *[Objective 4)*

3. Target Market

Describe the club's target market, as well as the size and characteristics of each segment within that market. Draw on any primary market research you have conducted, such as customer surveys, and any secondary research you have accessed.

- (Target 1)
- (Target 2)
- (Target 3)

3.1 Customer Profiles

Include profiles of the type of customers you are targeting. In each case, provide:

Customer Type	Demographics Gender, age, socio-economic grouping, occupations, location, etc.	Purchasing habits Control over purchasing decisions, previous sponsorship behaviour	Motivations Criteria for selecting product / service	Touchpoints Points of contact with customers (such as websites, social media, traditional media, etc.)
1				
2				
3				
4				
5				

3.2 Competitor Analysis

You should include details of your main competitors, and compare your product or service against those competitors. Identify the competitive advantages you believe your product or service (your club activities, facilities, etc.) has against these competitors.

4. Market Channels

Outline the channels you propose to use to reach and influence your target audience. Provide a summary of the marketing and communications activities you propose to conduct throughout the course of the period.

Appendix 17. Marketing Plan

Channel	Target Audience	Market / Communication Activity
1		
2		
3		
4		
5		

5. Implementation

For each marketing objective, you should:

- *List a range of actions that will be required to meet these objectives;*
- *List the metrics by which the objective will be measured;*
- *Set out a budget requirement;*
- *Identify the timeframe.*

Identify who will be responsible for these actions.

Objectives	Metrics	Budget	Timeframe	Responsibility
1				
2				
3				
4				

6. Some General Notes:

- Every club needs a consistent "sales message" (as against various members taking individual action) within its local sphere of activity.
- Clubs should understand that they are in a marketplace and that competition (from every other club in every other code in the area) will always be stiff.
- Get ahead of other clubs by having a marketing plan and be in a position to impress potential sponsors / benefactors with a coherent approach.
- Approaches to multinationals and other large entities need to be supported by positive documentation – a marketing plan / business plan fills that gap.
- Use every angle possible in the "7 Ps" of marketing to sell the club in the most attractive way.
- Convince the doubters that a marketing plan is a necessary tool for the club!

Appendix 18: Planning an Event

As described in **Chapter 12**, planning a major club event is a considerable undertaking. Working from the scenario below, this Appendix shows how to put into practice the guidance from the earlier text.

Scenario

Your club is a very large GAA club situated on a 14-acre site which sits 2 km outside a large town in Leinster. It is a club with a strong competitive record ranging over many years and which fields football, hurling and camogie teams at both senior level and at all age grades.

The club has well developed facilities and possesses a large clubhouse that includes a licenced bar. There is a large playing membership and a parallel membership of older members who can avail of a variety of social activities that run on a daily basis on the club premises.

The operation of a club of such size and range of activities creates a financial challenge from year to year. There is a strong record of fundraising but other clubs in the area are now challenging the marketplace with similar fundraising events. The general business environment indicates that finding significant sponsors has become much more difficult.

Discussion at General Committee level has centred around finding an event that could become a solid annual fundraiser and synonymous with the club. It has now been decided that the club's premises is ideal for a huge "Family Fete" to be run around mid-Summer.

Great idea – but who is going to lead it? You have previously run various events in the club so you are asked to lead this project. How will you go about realising the club's ambitions in this case?

Appendix 18. Planning an Event

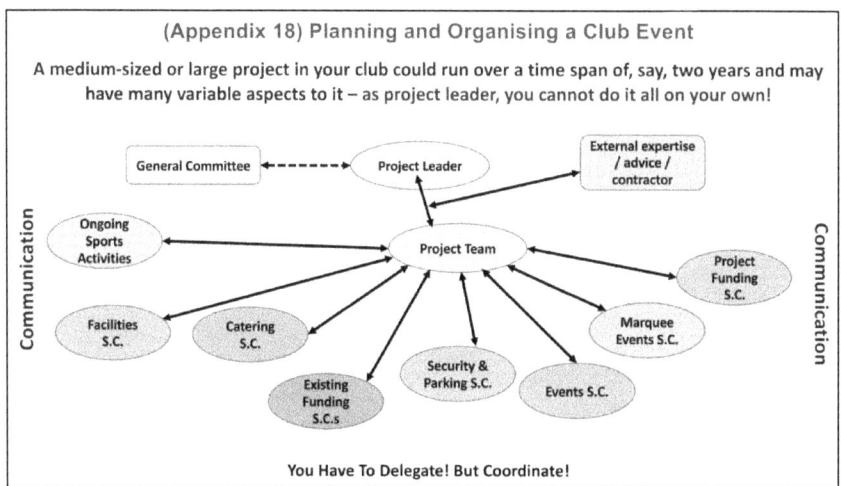

First thoughts

A medium-sized or large project in your club could run over several years and may have many variables. As project leader, you cannot do it all on your own. You will have to delegate – to a project team, to sub-committees, etc

Before even selecting a sub-committee, the project leader needs to have some initial thoughts on what the scope of this event should be:

- Will it be just a "family day" to be run over the course of a Sunday afternoon? Would such an event raise the amount of money required and would it be robust enough to become an annual event?
- Should it be a major, "split" event, a family day in the afternoon and, that evening, a concert with several live bands?
- Will the clubhouse cater for the numbers of guests who will have to be invited? If there was to be a "celebrity match", how would all those extra people be catered for?
- If such numbers were to be involved, would there be a need for a marquee? How would the expense of a marquee be met? If a marquee was necessary, could the expense be met by using it for a disco on the Saturday night?
- If there was to be live music, could a stage and sound system be hired? What period of time is needed to book some big-name bands? If there were some big-name bands, would there be a need for online ticketing? What is the ability of our website to do that?
- How would a balance be achieved between a meal for numerous guests, a celebrity match, a host of fete events, an evening concert (all of this having cleaned up after the disco)? Insurance costs? Who will clean up on Monday?

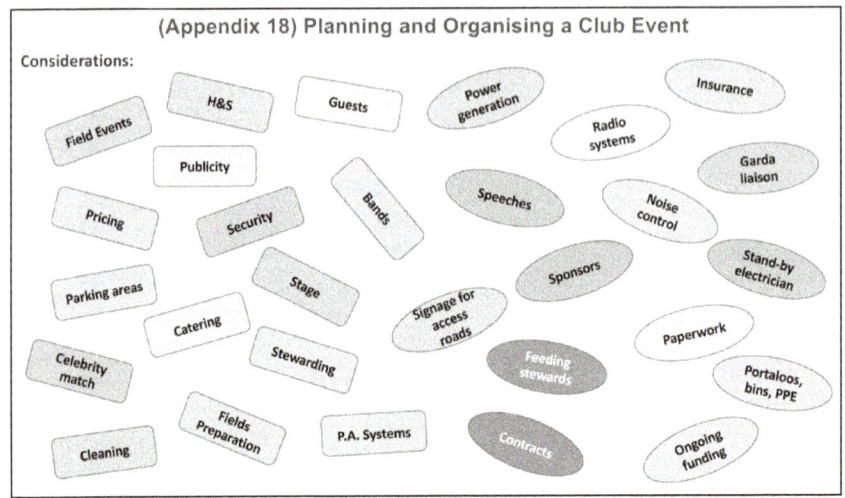

There will be a myriad of questions, so – more thoughts:
- The balance between the scope of the event, the effort involved and the money to be made has to be worked out. So, the objectives here have to be clearly defined.
- The long-term questions have to be answered first – for example, if the concert is to be approved, booking of bands, equipment, etc., needs to commence one year ahead.
- Some administrative questions (it's not all operations!) also need early clarification – will your insurance permit all of this and, if so, will there be a significant jump in premium? NEVER consider going ahead without informing your insurers.
- Understand what is "urgent", "important", etc. – this helps to put the appropriate focus on various elements and also helps to impose a sequence on the flow of preparations – sequence is important.
- Don't fret over any one element – if it is decided to hire a marquee, make the decision to make the best use of it – it could turn out to be a money-spinner. Make the decision and move on to the next decision.
- Put the major pieces of the jigsaw in place on paper (celebrity match / field events / concert / use of marquee) so that there is now an initial document in place for discussion with a sub-committee.
- It does not all have to be worked out but, having a skeletal plan in mind may help in selecting particular people for the sub-committee.

Even more thoughts:
- A detailed plan is not yet required – the project leader is not going to present the event sub-committee with a *fait accompli* – but, equally, the project leader is not going to open the discussion with a blank sheet and seek suggestions – this would result in a lot of "blue sky" thinking and a lot of time-wasting.
- The project leader will present a few major elements of the proposed event – subsequent discussion will add various other items to enhance the event – if,

Appendix 18. Planning an Event

- after discussion, one of the major planks of the event is removed, then that should be replaced with an alternative element.
- The project leader will have been careful in choosing the sub-committee. After the initial discussion it may become clear that other expertise / experience is required – this can be added but the sub-committee should not become too big. A second meeting of the sub-committee should provide enough material to produce an initial plan.
- The timing of the event requires careful thought – the calendar should be carefully considered to avoid possible clashes with other major events, be they local or national.
- The provisional plan should then be put to the General Committee in the form of a presentation, with documentation being issued to all General Committee members prior to the briefing meeting – this should mitigate against any major issues arising on the occasion.
- Some changes may be suggested by the General Committee and the sub-committee should be flexible enough to this on board – major changes should be avoided if the project leader unofficially briefs General Committee members prior to the official occasion.

On the assumption that the General Committee will give the green light to the provisional plan, the following must be quickly considered and actioned where necessary:

- The event sub-committee now has authority vested in it by the General Committee of the club – however, the sub-committee must now consider the ongoing activities in the club, the actions of other sub-committees and other fund-raising efforts.
- The sub-committee should review its make-up and ensure that it has the required experience and expertise to carry out its mandate. It should avoid becoming too large (6 or 7 people) and use smaller "task-teams" to carry out specific jobs, particularly as the event draws nearer.
- The sub-committee should have its own "officers" – the project leader will act as Chair while there will be need for a very competent Secretary and an astute Treasurer. A really good PRO is necessary unless the club PRO is good enough to do this. Ready access to and influence over the club website will be an added bonus.
- The immediate task will be to transform the provisional plan into the operational plan for the event. This will require a review of the mission statement and objectives and a determination that the skeletal plan was actually in line with such objectives.
- One of the main objectives will be to target the desired amount of money to be made from this event – this can be assessed after each separate element (field events, disco, concert, etc., etc.) is costed and a (conservative) profit is forecast. The methodology here should be documented, i.e. should there be an overall entry fee for the afternoon or should it be free entry with payment to enter / attend the various field events (carnival / vintage cars, etc.)

Keep going!
- The event sub-committee should finalise its operational plan as soon as possible and then prioritise the tasks which have the longest lead-time (booking a big-name band, assessing insurance implications, etc.).

- The project leader should guard against becoming too engrossed in any particular activity but should delegate as many tasks as possible and oversee, through review meetings, how matters are progressing. Persons with particular expertise can be co-opted onto the sub-committee to address particular items and can then stand down.
- The sub-committee itself should guard against being swamped by small tasks – these small tasks will multiply as the event comes into view and should be farmed out. However, the detail involved in making a planned event work can be quite minute and this needs to be documented in the operational plan, which can have detailed appendices attached as time progresses.
- There should be ongoing assessment of the manpower required to steward this event – because there will be "standing costs" (for example, marquee, stage, etc.) it would make sense to "sweat these assets" to make more money (so, if the marquee was erected on a Friday morning, every effort should be made to use it on Friday, Saturday and Sunday nights) for the event. Therefore, stewards will be required for three nights and all the activities involved over the weekend – this will take a lot of stewarding resources and will need planning – the General Committee and all sections of the club will be required to help out here.
- As the amount of detail and the variety of tasks grows, the importance of a solid, detailed operational plan will become more evident – trying to do this "off the cuff" could have severely negative, and costly, outcomes.

Keep thinking!

As said, there will be a multiplicity of tasks – these can only be managed properly on the day if there is proper support planning – otherwise the sub-committee will spend several days in fire-fighting a precarious situation. Small tasks must be documented – then that task can be given to the "task leader" in documented form – this avoids a lot of discussion and prevents confusion.

Take the task of parking – a seemingly simple task that can be forgotten – this event could involve in excess of 1,500 cars. Consider:

- The club can accommodate only 60 cars. What about the other 1,500? Parking for those with machinery / equipment?
- Can we get a local farmer to provide a field? How do we avoid damaging that field? How many stewards?
- Parking plan for field? Separate entry / exit points? How to get people safely from field to club? Shuttle bus?
- Separate teams of stewards for parking in club, parking in field, managing traffic from field to club?
- How long will each parking team be in place? Will they need refreshments? Will they need radio contact?
- Parking teams to serve all day / broken into shifts for afternoon / evening? How many Hi-Viz jackets?
- Permits from Garda / coordinate traffic with Garda? Tow truck for emergencies?
- More than one field location required? What are the implications for parking teams? What if it's wet?

Appendix 18. Planning an Event

- Briefing for all parking teams – when / who? What about cars being parked outside designated areas?
- Club insurance / farmers' insurance? Formal application to farmer(s). Free entry passes for those farmers?
- Traffic management in the dark after concert? Lighting at entry / exit. Torches for stewards?
- Traffic plan for access roads? How much directional signage? Internal signage in car-parks?
- Portaloo' in parking areas?
- Clean-up of farm field(s) on Monday? Disposal of rubbish? Debrief of task-leaders? Unforeseen costs?

Keep on planning!
- The devil is in the detail here – good planning should reveal a lot of the details.
- Take the initial "timeline" and, with more knowledge now, update that timeline.
- Fix (in terms of planning, contracts, applications, etc.) the four or five big issues (marquee / bands / carnival, etc.) to be addressed on the timeline – the major planks are now in place and detailed work to make these happen can now commence.
- Now commence adding in smaller events and how they will be addressed – start building the tapestry that will make up a very full event.
- Particular events might take more organising time (e.g. getting a "celebrity" team to play the club team) – give such a task to a particular person and monitor progress
- Continue to update and amend the operational plan as the various pieces become more clear – "support" activities (for example, car-parking) should be outlined and placed in an appendix at the back of the plan – when the time comes this appendix can be detached as a stand-alone document and given to the car-parking task leader.
- The difference between having a very successful, and profitable, event or having a half-baked effort that will frustrate everybody and not make a lot of money is having a well-considered and detailed plan.

Again, when it's all over, write up a comprehensive review of the overall operation and add in any pertinent documents as appendices – present this to the General Committee for the record. Remember – somebody else may have to do this next year – no point in reinventing the wheel!

Remember Administration

Planning and organising a major club event usually focuses on "getting things done" – making sure all the planned activities occur as expected. However, it is equally important that operational actions are properly supported by administrative actions. As we've seen earlier in this book, good administration is the backbone of any operation – it both authenticates actions and provides a verifiable record in the wake of events.

Such administrative support could include:

- Correspondence with insurers;
- Contracts with performers;
- Applications for permits (Garda, etc.);
- Correspondence with (say) farmers for parking, etc.;
- Notification about the event to nearby dwellings;
- Invitations to guests;
- Correspondence with Local Authority;
- Minutes of all sub-committee meetings;
- Applications for sponsorship;
- Correspondence with particular participants;
- Notifications to club members;
- Creation of folders on various laptops;
- Invitations to politicians and officers of NGBs;
- Explanatory responses to various queries;
- Letters of appreciation to appropriate parties.

These are just some examples. The staging of a club event can generate a deal of paperwork, depending on its structure and nature. A well-organised, self-driven Secretary will be a vital asset!

The headings for an event operation plan might include:

1. Club Development Background
2. Outline of Event
3. Mission Statement
4. Event Objectives
5. Preparation Timeline
6. Event Sub-committee
7. Event Activities
8. Club Involvement
9. Administration
10. Appendices
    - Preparation Timeline
    - Task teams
    - Ground Activities Plan
    - Car park Plan
    - Stewarding Plan
    - Catering Plan
    - Operation of Marquee
    - Ticketing Operation
    - Concert Operation

Appendix 18. Planning an Event

To monitor operations, you could use a Excel spreadsheet set up like this:

(Appendix 18) Sample Headings for Monitoring of Operations Plan

ABC [Sport] Club – Operations Plan for Family Fete – July 20XX

Activity	Responsibility	Start Date	Particular Timings	Particular Actions	Review Dates	Further Actions	Closure
Grounds Layout Plan							
Fete Activities Plan							
Concert Plan							
Match Plan							
Marketing Plan							
Ticketing Plan							
Safety Plan							
Parking Plan							
Contingencies							
Stewarding							
Catering Plan							
Administration							

ABOUT THE AUTHOR

J.J. Killian, MBA, FCIPD, FCILT is a former army officer, businessman and organisational management consultant who has been involved in sport and sports clubs for all of his life. He has played most sports and, unlike many of those who play, he has taken many opportunities to appreciate what has to happen off-pitch to ensure that games can be played on-pitch and enjoyed in a positive environment.

His on-pitch activities have always been mirrored by an involvement in the administration of the clubs in which he has been involved. This sports administration involvement has been matched by many years of service on Boards of Directors, National Councils, Boards of Voluntary Organisations and other committees. The experience gathered in such organisational structures is now relayed through this handbook which should provide valuable support to any person involved in the administration of sports clubs. J.J.'s extensive involvement with committees and boards is outlined here:

- National:
  - Member of National Council of ISME for 18 years. Chairman for 2 years.
  - Sitting Member of Employment Appeals Tribunal (EAT) for 10 years.
- Professional:
  - Member of Board (MD) of Flancare Distribution (Clonmel) Ltd. for 17 years.

- Member of National Council of CILT for two years. Chartered Fellow, CILT.
  - Chartered Fellow of CIPD for 18 years.
- Sports:
  - Member of General Committee, Hillview Sports Club, Clonmel for 10 years. Tennis Captain for 1 year.
  - Member of General Committee, Clonmel Athletic Club for four years.
  - President, Kickham Squash Club, Clonmel for 5 years.
  - Member of General Committee of The Island Squash Club for 5 years.
  - Member of General Committee of Clonmel Rugby Club for over 30 years. Served as Chairperson of club for 5 years, Finance & Development Chairperson for 7 years and Director of Rugby for 2 years. Served as President for 2 years.
- Arts & Culture:
  - Member of Board of Directors, Clonmel Junction Arts Festival for 2 years.
  - Member of General Committee, Fleadh Cheoil, Clonmel for 3 years.
- Community:
  - Member and Officer of Clonmel Lions Club for 20 years. President for 1 year and a Melvin Jones Fellow.
  - Chairperson of Residents' Association for 3 years (ongoing).
  - Chairperson of Group Sewerage Scheme for 1 year (ongoing).

J.J. has advised governing bodies and many sports clubs on matters such as governance, structure, strategy and operational systems. He has held office at every level in a range of clubs so he has extensive experience of the operations of clubs and the issues they face. He has also created and delivered the Level 6 Special Purpose Certificate Course, "Sports Club Administration" for Limerick Institute of Technology (LIT) and Tipperary Sports Partnership (TSP). J.J. has written extensively for local papers on topics ranging from sports reporting to articles relating to countries in which he has worked. He continues to lecture at LIT and to advise sports clubs on practical operational issues.

OAK TREE PRESS

Oak Tree Press develops and delivers information, advice and resources for entrepreneurs and managers. It is Ireland's leading business book publisher, with an unrivalled reputation for quality titles across business, management, HR, law, marketing and enterprise topics.

In addition, Oak Tree Press occupies a unique position in start-up and small business support in Ireland through its standard-setting titles, as well training courses, mentoring and advisory services.

Oak Tree Press is comfortable across a range of communication media – print, web and training, focusing always on the effective communication of business information.

OAK TREE PRESS
E: info@oaktreepress.com
W: www.oaktreepress.com / www.SuccessStore.com.

www.ingramcontent.com/pod-product-compliance
Lightning Source LLC
Chambersburg PA
CBHW071204160426
43196CB00011B/2197